DATE			
MAY 17 1984			
JUL 02 1984			
AUG 2 1988			
FEB 5 1990			
JUL 5 1991			
MAY 5 '92			
JUN 29 '93			
SEP 30 '93			
OCT 04 '94			
APR 20 '95			
MAY 9 '95			

FOR THE STORY TELLER

FOR
THE STORY TELLER

STORY TELLING AND STORIES TO TELL

BY

CAROLYN SHERWIN BAILEY

1913

MILTON BRADLEY COMPANY

SPRINGFIELD, MASS.

Republished by Gale Research Company, Detroit, Michigan, 1971

Library of Congress Cataloging in Publication Data

Bailey, Carolyn Sherwin, 1875-1961.
  For the story teller.

  Reprint of the ed. published by M. Bradley Co.,
Springfield, Mass.
    Bibliography: p.
    1. Story-telling. 2. Children's stories.
I. Title.
LB1042.B3   1975   372.6'4   74-23576
ISBN 0-8103-3802-5

PREFACE

THE new-old art of story telling is being rediscovered. We are finding that the children's daily story hour in school, in the neighborhood house, and at home is a real force for mental and moral good in their lives. We are learning that it is possible to educate children by means of stories.

Story telling to be a developing factor in a child's life must be studied by the story teller. There are good stories and there are poor stories for children. The story that fits a child's needs to-day may not prove a wise choice for him to-morrow. Some stories teach, some stories only give joy, some stories inspire, some stories just make a child laugh. Each of these story phases is important. To discover these special types of stories, to fit stories to the individual child or child group, and to make over stories for perfect telling has been my aim in writing this book.

PREFACE

Through telling stories to many thousands of children and lecturing to students I have found that story telling is a matter of psychology. The pages that follow give my new theory of story telling to the teacher or parent.

CAROLYN SHERWIN BAILEY.

CONTENTS

vii

CONTENTS

FOR THE STORY TELLER

CHAPTER I

THE APPERCEPTIVE BASIS OF STORY TELLING

APPERCEPTION is a formidable and sometimes confusing term for a very simple and easy-to-understand mental process. I once told Seumus MacManus' deliciously humorous story of Billy Beg and his Bull to a group of foreign boys and girls in one of New York's East Side Settlement Houses. The children listened with apparent appreciation, but, halfway along in the story, it occurred to me to ask them if they had ever seen a bull. No one answered me at first. Then Pietro, a little dusky-eyed son of Italy, raised a grimy hand.

"I seen one last summer when we was on a *fresh-air,*" he said. "It's a bigger cow, a bull is, with the bicycle handle-bars on her head."

Pietro's description of a bull was an example

of apperception, the method by means of which a new idea is interpreted, classified, "let into" the human mind. He knew the class, *cows*. He also knew the class, *bicycles*. He did not know the class, *bulls*—at least vividly enough to be able to put the idea into terms of a verbal explanation and description. So he did the most natural thing in the world, the only possible mental process in fact by means of which children or adults classify the *new*. He interpreted it in terms of the old, explaining the unfamiliar idea, bull, by means of the familiar ideas, cow and a bicycle.

This, then, is apperception. *It is the involuntary mental process by means of which the human mind makes its own the strange, the new, the unfamiliar idea by a method of fitting it into the class of familiar ideas already known.* Apperception is a means of quick mental interpretation. It is the welcoming of strangers to the mind-habitation, strangers who come every day in the guise of unfamiliar names, terms, scenes, and phrases, and determining in which corner of the brain house they will fit most comfortably. The most natural process is finally to give these new ideas an old mind corner to rest in, or an old brain path in which to travel.

A child's mind at the age when he is able to concentrate upon listening to a story, three or four years of age—kindergarten age—is not a very crowded house. It is a mind-house tenanted by a few and very simple concepts which he has made his own through his previous home, mother and play experiences. He is familiar with his nursery, his pets, his family, his toys, his food, his bed. If he is a country child he knows certain flowers, birds and farm animals, not as classes—flower, bird and animal—but as *buttercup, robin* and *sheep*. If he is a city child his mind has a very different tenantry, and he thinks in terms of *street, subway, park, fire engine, ambulance*. These to the city child are also individual ideas, not classes. He knows them as compelling, noisy, moving ideas which he has seen and experienced, but they do not at all appeal to him as classes.

The story of "The Three Bears" is an obviously interesting one to children upon entering school. It has its basis of interest in its apperceptive quality, and it illustrates better than almost any other story for children those qualities which bring about quick mental interpretation on the part of the listener. The unusual, strange, hazardous characters in the story, the three bears, are introduced to the child in old, comfortably familiar terms which catch his interest from the first sentence of the story. It is extremely doubtful if the story of three bears set in a polar or forest environment would ever have been popular so long or made so many children happy as has the story of the historical three bears who lived in a house, ate porridge from bowls, sat in chairs and slept in beds. Nor are these the only apperceptive links between the life of the bears and that of the child. There is a tiny bear in the story, the size, one may presuppose, of the child who is listening to the story. The to-be-classified idea, *bear,* is presented to children in this old folk tale in terms of already known ideas, *house, porridge, chair, bed* and *tiny.* Very few story tellers have appreciated the underlying psychologic appeal of the story of "The Three Bears," but it illustrates a quality in stories that we must look for if we wish to make the story we select a permanency in the child's mental life.

The apperceptive basis of story telling consists in study on the part of the story teller to discover what is the store of ideas in the minds of the children who will listen to the story.

Has the story too many new ideas for the child to be able to classify them in terms of his old ideas? On the other hand, has it one or two new thoughts so carefully presented through association with already familiar concepts that the child will be able to make them his own and give them a permanent place in his mind with the old ones?

A child's mind is an eery place for an adult to try and enter. Teachers, kindergartners and story tellers are a little prone to think that a knowledge of one child's mental content gives them the power to know the mind of the child-at-large. Our psychologists have given us studies of child mind, not child minds. This mind hypothesis is, perhaps, sufficient for the general working out of systems of teaching, but success in the delicate art of story telling means a most critical study and observation of the minds of the special group of children who will hear the story. The story teller must ask herself these questions:

"What do these children *know?*"

"Have they any experience other than that of the home on which to bank?"

"Do they come from homes of leisure or homes of industry?"

"Have they had a country or a city experience?"

"Have they passed from the stage of development when toys formed their play interest to the game stage in which chance and hazard interest them more deeply?"

"Are they American children, familiar with American institutions, or are they little aliens in our land, unfamiliar with and confused by our ways?"

When she has satisfactorily answered these questions, the story teller will select her story having for its theme, atmosphere and *motif* an idea or group of ideas that will touch the child's mental life as she has discovered it and by means of which it will find a permanent place in his mind through its comfortable friendliness and familiarity.

The child who has come directly from his home and the sheltering arms of his mother or nurse should not, at first, be taken far afield through the lands of fairies and giants. If he is told a fairy story, it should have for its content the sweet, homely qualities that characterize the home. I am using as a good example of the apperceptive story, "The Cap that Mother Made." The child listeners are carried, it is true, to the palace of a King and are formally introduced to a Princess, but this is brought about through the familiar symbols of the home: *mother, brothers,* the *farmer,* and the queer little *cap* with its red and green stripes and blue tassel. Although Anders, the story hero, spends a happy hour at the Princess' ball, he finally finds his way home again, and the story has an apperceptive appeal which is unusual. It is full of precious, familiar concepts that establish an association in the child's mind between fairyland and home. After hearing the story, he will be very apt always to remember a palace as a very charming place to visit, but not to stay in, when one may go home to mother.

THE CAP THAT MOTHER MADE

Once upon a time there was a little boy named Anders, who had a new cap. And a prettier cap you never have seen, for mother herself had knit it; and nobody could make anything quite so nice as mother did. It was altogether red, except a small part in the middle which was green, for the red yarn had given out; and the tassel was blue.

His brothers and sisters walked about squinting at him, and their faces grew long with envy. But Anders cared nothing about that. He put his hands in his pockets and went out for a walk, for he wished everybody to see how fine he looked in his new cap.

The first person he met was a farmer walking along by the side of a wagon load of wood. He made a bow so deep that his back came near breaking. He was dumbfounded, I can tell you, when he saw it was nobody but Anders.

"Dear me," said he, "if I did not think it was the gracious little count himself!" And then he invited Anders to ride in his wagon.

8

But when one has a pretty, red cap with a blue tassel, one is too fine to ride in a wagon, and Anders walked proudly by.

At the turn of the road he met the tanner's son, Lars. He was such a big boy that he wore high boots, and carried a jack-knife. He gaped and gazed at the cap, and could not keep from fingering the blue tassel.

"Let's trade caps," he said. "I will give you my jack-knife to boot."

Now this knife was a very good one, though half the blade was gone and the handle was a little cracked; and Anders knew that one is almost a man as soon as one has a jack-knife. But still it did not come up to the new cap which mother had made.

"Oh, no, I'm not so stupid as all that; no, I'm not!" Anders said.

And then he said good-by to Lars with a nod; but Lars only made faces at him, for he had not been to school much, poor boy; and, besides, he was very much put out because he could not cheat Anders out of his cap which mother had made.

Anders went along, and he met a very old, old woman who courtesied till her skirts looked like a balloon. She called him a little gentleman, and said that he was fine enough to go to the royal court ball.

"Yes, why not?" thought Anders. "Seeing that I am so fine, I may as well go and visit the King."

And so he did. In the palace yard stood two soldiers with shining helmets, and with muskets over their shoulders; and when Anders came to the gate, both the muskets were leveled at him.

"Where may you be going?" asked one of the soldiers.

"I am going to the court ball," answered Anders.

"No, you are not," said the other soldier, stepping forward. "Nobody is allowed there without a uniform."

But just at this instant the princess came tripping across the yard. She was dressed in white silk with bows of gold ribbon. When she saw Anders and the soldiers, she walked over to them.

"Oh," she said, "he has such a very fine cap on his head, and that will do just as well as a uniform."

And she took Anders' hand and walked with him up the broad marble stairs where soldiers were posted at every third step, and through the beautiful halls where courtiers in silk and velvet stood bowing wherever he went. For no doubt they thought him a prince when they saw his fine cap.

At the farther end of the largest hall a table was set with golden cups and golden plates in long rows. On huge silver dishes were piles of tarts and cakes, and red wine sparkled in shining glasses.

The princess sat down at the head of this long table; and she let Anders sit in a golden chair by her side.

"But you must not eat with your cap on your head," she said, putting out her hand to take it off.

"Oh, yes, I can eat just as well," said Anders, holding on to his cap; for if they should take it away from him nobody would any longer believe that he was a prince; and, besides, he did not feel sure that he would get it back again.

"Well, well, give it to me," said the princess, "and I will give you a kiss."

The princess was certainly beautiful, and Anders would have dearly liked to be kissed by her, but the cap which mother had made he would not give up on any condition. He only shook his head.

"Well, but see," said the princess; and she filled his pockets with cakes, and put her own gold chain around his neck, and bent down and kissed him.

But he only moved farther back in his chair and did not take his hands away from his head.

Then the doors were thrown open, and the King entered with a large number of gentlemen in glittering uniforms and plumed hats. The King himself wore a purple mantle which trailed behind him, and he had a large gold crown on his white curly hair.

He smiled when he saw Anders in the gilt chair.

"That is a very fine cap you have," he said.

"So it is," replied Anders. "Mother knit it of her very best yarn, and everybody wishes to get it away from me."

"But surely you would like to change caps with me," said the King, raising his large, heavy crown from his head.

Anders did not answer. He sat as before, and held on to his red cap which everybody was so eager to get. But when the King came nearer to him, with his gold crown between his hands, then Anders grew frightened as never before. If he did not take good care, the King might cheat him out of his cap; for a King can do whatever he likes.

With one jump Anders was out of his chair. He darted like an arrow through all the beautiful halls, down all the marble stairs, and across the yard.

He twisted himself like an eel between the outstretched arms of the courtiers, and over the soldiers' muskets he jumped like a little rabbit.

He ran so fast that the princess's necklace fell off his neck, and all the cakes jumped out of his pockets. But his cap he still had. He was holding on to it with both hands as he rushed into his mother's cottage.

His mother took him up in her lap, and he told her all his adventures, and how everybody wanted his cap. And all his brothers and sisters stood around and listened with their mouths open.

But when his big brother heard that he had refused to give his cap for the King's golden crown, he said that Anders was stupid. Just think how much money one might get for the King's crown; and Anders could have had a still finer cap.

That Anders had not thought of, and his face grew red. He put his arms around his mother's neck and asked:

"Mother, was I stupid?"

His mother hugged him close and kissed him.

"No, my little son," said she. "If you were

dressed in silver and gold from top to toe, you could not look any nicer than in your little red cap."

Then Anders felt brave again. He knew well enough that mother's cap was the best cap in all the world.

From Swedish Fairy Tales.

This story is only an example of many others that may be selected and fitted to the mental status of the individual child or group of children who make up the story circle. I had great difficulty one season in gaining and holding the attention of a group of particularly rough boys to whom I was telling stories in a neighborhood house. To my surprise, they listened most attentively to an adaptation of "The King of the Golden River," and clamored to have it repeated. Looking into the reason for their keen interest in the story, which really took them quite far afield in its descriptions and plot, I discovered that the incident of the holy water had gripped my audience. The boys were Romanists and they found a point in the story which touched their own lives, in the visits of the brothers and

Gluck to the priest. I never afterward found difficulty in holding the attention of this special group of boys. I had been able to establish a bond of sympathy between the boys and the story characters.

Touching a child's life through the medium of a story is like a friendly hand clasp. An Irish folk tale told to a group of little sons and daughters of Erin, one of the Uncle Remus tales told to a kindergarten circle of little negroes, the story of one of our Italian operas adapted to the understanding of Sicilian and Neapolitan children, one and all mean enriching those child lives. How could the Gaelic tale fit the Italian group, though, or the story of the opera make an appeal to the little negro boys and girls?

Successful story telling means, then, a careful consideration of the apperceptive basis of the story, first of all. This, reduced to very simple terms, means studying the mental life of a child and selecting for his first stories those that have a well-defined association through their word pictures, dialogue and plot with the child's own previous experience.

When the story teller makes the question of apperception the first consideration in selecting her stories, she will find that her appeal to the children will be an active and successful one.

Goody Two Shoes

SELECTED FOR ITS APPERCEPTIVE APPEAL

Of course Goody Two Shoes was not her real name. In fact, her father's name was Meanwell, and he had once been rich, and prosperous, and one of the most well-to-do farmers in the parish, but he lost his money. However it happened one could hardly tell, but his farm was seized, and he was turned out with his wife, and Tommy, and little Marjery, with none of the necessaries of life to support them.

Care and discontent shortened the days of Farmer Meanwell. He was forced from his family and taken with a violent fever of which he died. Marjery's poor mother died soon, too, of a broken heart, and Marjery and her little brother were left alone in the wide world; so they started off together, hand in hand, to seek their fortunes.

They were both very ragged, and though Tommy had two shoes, Marjery had but one. They neither had anything to support them save what they picked from the hedges, or got from the poor people; and they slept every night in a barn. Their relations, who were rich folk, took no notice of them, because they were ashamed to own such a poor little ragged girl as Marjery and such a dirty little curly-pated boy as Tommy.

But there was a very worthy clergyman named Mr. Smith who lived in the parish where little Marjery and Tommy were born; and having a relation come to see him who was a charitable man, he sent for these children. The gentleman ordered little Marjery a new pair of shoes, gave Mr. Smith some money to buy them clothes, and said he would take Tommy and make of him a little sailor. He had a new jacket and trousers made for Tommy, and he was soon ready to start for London.

It was hard indeed for Tommy and Marjery to part. Tommy cried, and Marjery cried, and they kissed each other a hundred times. At last Tommy wiped off Marjery's tears with the end of his jacket and bid her cry no more, for he would come to her again when he returned from sea, and he began his journey with the kind gentleman while Marjery went crying to bed. And the instant that Marjery awoke the next morning, the shoemaker came in with the new shoes for which she had been measured.

Nothing could have helped little Marjery bear the loss of Tommy more than the pleasure she took in her two shoes. You remember she had worn only one shoe before, and a ragged one at that. She ran out to Mrs. Smith as soon as they were put on, and stroking down her ragged apron cried out, "Two shoes, Madam, see, two shoes!" And so she behaved to all the people she met, and she obtained the name of Goody Two Shoes.

With Tommy gone there was not a great deal for Goody Two Shoes to do, so she made up her mind that she would learn to read. Now in the long ago days when this little girl lived, one had to pay quite a sum of money to go to a dame's school and be taught how to cross stitch, and to bow politely, and to read. Only rich children could go, but Goody Two Shoes would meet the little boys and girls as they came from school, and learn from them and then sit down and read until they returned. After a while she had taught herself more than they had learned of the dame, and she resolved to go the rounds of all the farms and teach the little children who were too poor to go to school.

And such a clever, pleasant way of teaching children to read as Goody Two Shoes invented! With her knife she cut some wooden sets of letters with which the children were to spell and make sentences by laying them together. These wooden letters she put in a basket and with the basket over her arm she became a little trotting tutoress who was known through all the countryside for her kindness and patience.

Each morning she would start out at seven and run up to the door of a farmhouse.

Tap, tap, tap!

"Who is there?" the mother of the house would ask.

"Only little Goody Two Shoes," Marjery would answer, "come to teach Billy his A B C's."

"Oh, little Goody," the mother would cry, opening the door wide. "I am glad to see you. Billy wants you sadly, for he has learned all his lesson."

Little Billy would come out and have a new spelling lesson set him with the basket of letters, and then Goody would go on to Farmer Simpson's.

"Bow, wow, wow!" said the dog at the door.

"Sirrah," Mistress Simpson would say, "why

do you bark at Little Two Shoes? Come in. Here's Sally wants you sadly, for she has learned all her lesson."

Then out came the little one.

"Good morning, Goody," she would say.

"Good morning, Sally," Goody Two Shoes would answer; " have you learned your lesson?"

"Yes, that's what I have," the little one would say, as she took the letters and spelled *pear,* and *plum,* and *top,* and *ball,* and *puss,* and *cow,* and *lamb,* and *sheep,* and *bull,* and *cock,* and *hen.*

"Good," said Marjery, and she hurried on to Gaffer Cook's cottage. Here a number of poor children were met to learn to read and they all crowded around Marjery at once. So she pulled out her letters and asked the little boy next her what he had for dinner. He answered, *bread.*

"Well, then," said she, "set the first letter."

So he pulled out a big B, and soon the other letters, and there stood the word as plain as possible.

"And what had you, Polly Comb, for your dinner?" asked Goody Two Shoes.

"Apple-pie," answered Polly as she spelled her word.

The next child had potatoes, the next beef and turnips, which were spelled with many other

20

words until the lesson was done, and Goody set them a new task, and went on.

The next place she came to was Farmer Thompson's, where there were a great many little ones waiting for her.

"Oh, little Miss Goody Two Shoes," said one of them, "where have you been?"

"I have been teaching," said Goody, "longer than I intended, and am afraid I am come too soon for you now."

"No, but indeed you are not," replied the other, "for I have got my lesson, and so has Sally Dawson, and so have we all," and they capered about as if they were overjoyed to see her.

"Why, then," said she, "you are all very good; so let us begin our lessons."

She was indeed a wise and painstaking little tutoress for a long, long time. At last Dame Williams, who kept the village school for little gentlemen and ladies, became very old and infirm, and wanted to give up teaching. So the trustees sent for Little Two Shoes to examine her and see if she were able to keep the school.

They found that little Marjery was the best scholar and had the best heart of any one who wanted to be the teacher, and they gave her a most favorable report.

So Goody Two Shoes' troubles and travels were over. She taught the dame school for the rest of her days, and never lacked for shoes or anything else needful.

OLIVER GOLDSMITH, 1765.

Adapted.

STORIES SELECTED BECAUSE OF THEIR GENERAL AP-
PERCEPTIVE APPEAL TO A CHILD UPON EN-
TERING SCHOOL

THE HOUSE THAT JACK BUILT	*Mother Goose*
THE THREE BEARS	*Folk Tale*
THE THREE LITTLE PIGS	" "
LITTLE RED RIDING HOOD	" "
THE GOAT AND THE SEVEN LITTLE KIDS	" "
THE LITTLE RED HEN	" "
THE TOWN MOUSE AND THE COUNTRY MOUSE	*Æsop's Fables*
THE ELVES AND THE SHOEMAKER	*The Brothers Grimm*
THE TOP AND THE BALL	*Hans Christian Andersen*
HOW THE HOME WAS BUILT	*Maud Lindsay, in Mother Stories*
THE LITTLE GRAY GRANDMOTHER	
	Elizabeth Harrison, in Story Land
THE PIG BROTHER	*Laura E. Richards, in The Golden Windows*
GRANDFATHER'S PENNY	*In For the Children's Hour*
TINY TIM	*Adapted from Dickens, in For the Children's Hour*

Montessori, but the *sense story* has been completely overlooked. *We have made little effort to appeal to a child's mind through the story that has sense images of sight, touch, sound or taste to strengthen the mind impression which it makes.*

If we analyze the story that has interested us most in a current magazine, we shall discover that, somehow, it made a direct appeal to our senses. It may have had the setting of some old garden, the description of which made us, in imagination, smell the clove pinks, roses, French lilacs and mignonette that grew in some garden of our childhood. Perhaps it was a *sound* story, giving us such speaking word pictures of bird songs, violin tones or even the human notes of voices that we almost *heard* the story instead of seeing it. On the other hand, the sense appeal of the story may have been that of *color,* of *food*—any sense stimulus that routed from their brain corners our old sense impressions and set them to working again. And it is almost impossible to gauge the effect upon cerebration of these stored-up sensory images.

That whiff of odor from a city flower cart brings suddenly to my mind an incident that I had not been cognizant of for years—the memory of a certain long-ago day when I purloined my Grandmother's scissors and cut off two of my curls to make a wig for a hairless rag doll.   What is the connection between this day of badness of my childhood and a dingy city flower wagon?   Ah, I have it!   There was a pot of Martha Washington geraniums in the room where I sat when I cut my hair. My small, serge sleeve brushed the leaves as I held the curls triumphantly to the light and the pungent odor found a permanent place in my mind, side by side with the other memory, ineffaceable, always ready to produce a recall.

Dr. Van Dyke once said that if he were able to paint a picture of Memory, he would picture her asleep in a bed of mint.   He illustrated the value of sensory stimuli in fiction. One gauge of a perfectly constructed piece of fiction is its sense content.   Does it include such writing as will make the reader *see, taste, smell* and *hear?*   So, in stories for children we must apply the same test.

A child's story, to interest, should have a strong sense appeal.

Many of the old, handed-down jingles and folk tales are full of *eating* and *drinking,* *smelling* delectable odors, *hearing* the sounds of child life and *seeing* over again child scenes. Therein lies their world appeal and the reason for their ancient and obvious popularity.

"The Queen of Hearts,
   She made some *tarts.*"

"Little Tommy Tucker, *sings* for his *supper;*
   What shall he *eat? White bread and butter.*"

"*Ding, dong bell,* Pussy's in the well."

"Hark, hark, the dogs do *bark,*
   The beggars are coming to town."

"Rockaby baby, your cradle is *green.*"

"The rose is *red,*
   The violet *blue,*
   Sugar is *sweet*
   And so are you."

27

One might go on indefinitely quoting lines of Mother Goose that tickle a child's fancy and are undying in their appeal for the sole reason that they are sensual in the broader understanding of the term. They include simple, direct references to the mental concepts that the child has gained through his senses. Practically all that the normal, natural child has accomplished, mentally, up to the age of three or four years, has been to note bright colors, to handle everything he has come in contact with,—not, as so many persons suppose, for purposes of mischievous destruction, but rather to touch each object and make its feeling an integral part of his ego,—to eat and drink and to use his nostrils as a dog does. What more natural than that his beginnings in English should have for their basis a sense content that will help the child to *name,* put into words his previously acquired but unnamed sense impressions?

Miss Emilie Poulsson's finger plays for little children have for their basic appeal the stimulating of a child's ability to recall previously acquired sense impressions. In addition, the

finger movements with which the child illustrates these rhymes give the added association
of the sense of touch to strengthen and vivify
the child's interest in and memory of the rhyme
stories. To illustrate:

> "Here's a ball for baby,
> *Big* and *soft* and *round.*
>
> Here's the baby's hammer,
> Oh, how he can *pound.*
>
> Here's the baby's *music,*
> *Clapping, clapping* so.
>
> Here are baby's soldiers
> Standing in a row—"

As the child grows beyond the age when
Mother Goose and Finger Plays appeal to him,
he still finds his greatest interest in those stories
which stimulate his acquired sensory images.
The mental operation of apperception described in the last chapter is so inclusive a
process, covering, as it must of necessity,
memory and perception, that it explains the appeal of the sense story to the mind of a child.

29

Many of the stories quoted at the end of the chapter as being of universal interest to all children find their common points of interest in their sense pictures, so quickly grasped and so warmly welcomed by the child mind whose sense doors are always flung wide open.

It is to be questioned whether or not the story of "The Little Red Hen" would have been awarded such immortality if its heroine had been a plain *hen* and not *red*. Having been dyed with the crimson pigment of the imagination, however, by some old-world story teller, she has taken her cheerful, cackling way through the streets of childhood, an undying, classic fowl of fiction because she is colored. So it is with Elizabeth Harrison's wonderful allegory of "The Little Gray Grandmother." She might have been described in the story as a spirit, a fairy, a mythical character who influenced for good the lives of Wilhelm, Beata and the others. But instead of *describing* her invisibility—Miss Harrison *paints* it, colors her story heroine with the shades of intangible things. She is a little *gray* grandmother and her clothes are sea fog and her veil is of smoke.

She is an animated part of the seashore home and is made of gray mist. What could be more artistic than the sense appeal of this story?

Why do children—all children—listen, gaping and ecstatic, to the account of the many and hazardous adventures of the Gingerbread Boy? Why do they beg to have the story told over again, even after they have heard it so many times that they know it by heart. Its universal popularity is not due to its folklore quality. Neither is it due to its plot and treatment, although these undoubtedly strengthen it. Its big appeal, however, is to the child's sense of taste. The story arouses tasting images in the child's mind, that are pleasurable and strong.

. . . "A chocolate jacket and cinnamon seeds for buttons! His eyes were made of fine, fat currants; his mouth was made of rose-colored sugar and he had a gay little cap of orange-sugar candy"—Sara Cone Bryant says in describing her Gingerbread Man. So, from this delectable, luscious paragraph about his make-up, to the climax of the story when the Gingerbread Man is devoured by the fox, the child hearers *eat* in imagination all the way.

"Why the Chimes Rang" makes a different and more ethical sense appeal to the child's mind. The story stimulates in the listeners a deep interest in the old chime of bells that has hung silent for so long a time in the tower. One longs to hear them and waits anxiously for the miracle that will start their pealing. At the story climax, when an unselfish offering laid upon the altar works the wonder, it is possible to listen, in imagination, to the bells' sweet music.

But why make this sense appeal to the child mind through the medium of a story, the story teller asks?

There are two very real and definite uses to which the sense story may be put.

Such sense stories as "The Little Red Hen," "The Gingerbread Boy" and many others of similar character may be told not only to give pleasure to the child of kindergarten age who finds delight in their sensual content, but they have a very real value in *resurrecting the dormant brain of a mentally deficient child.* More and more attention is being given every year to the education of the feeble-minded child, both at home and in the public schools. We are discovering that it is possible to rouse to action a child's sleeping brain by means of intensive sense training. We are teaching him to smell, taste, see color, discriminate forms and textiles, to open the telegraphic circuit of his senses. We are putting the world of realities into the arms of the feeble-minded child to touch, feel, taste, smell, see. So we educate him, but we must carry out the same system of sense training in his stories, selecting for his hearing those stories that make verbal and recall his previously acquired sense impressions.

There is one other use to which we may put the sense story. *It is a means of strengthening any child's imagination.* The same mental operation by means of which a baby associates the idea *cold* with a block of ice, helps the child to feel the cold of Andersen's "Little Match Girl." In the first instance the association of *cold* and ice means self-preservation for the baby. He wishes to avoid an unpleasant sensation, so he does not touch the ice, but his former experience of touching it has left an ineffaceable image in his mind. In the second instance, the image *cold* is recalled in the mind of the child by the story and the result is a very different mental process. The child is able through the sensory stimulus of the story to feel with the little match girl, to put himself in her place, to understand her condition, because it is brought to him in a familiar term—*cold*.

The story teller who makes the wisest use of the sense story sees to it that the color, sound, taste or odor described in the story is used as a *means to an end*. One does not wish to stimulate sense images in a child's mind for the simple operation of "making his thinking machine work" in old paths. What we must do is to utilize his sense impressions to strengthen new brain paths. Fortunately nearly all of the stories for children that have a sensory content utilize this mode of writing to strengthen the climax of the story. It only remains for the story teller to select her *color, sound, taste, odor* or *touch* story to meet the special needs of her children. The following story is an excellent illustration of utilizing the sense of taste to point a moral:

THE THREE CAKES

Once upon a time there was a little boy named Henry, who was away from his home at a boarding school.

He was a very special kind of boy, forever at his book, and he happened once to get to the very tip top of his class. His mother was told of it, and when it came morning, she got up early and went to speak with the cook as follows:

"Cook, you are to make a cake for Henry, who has been very good at school."

"With all my heart," said the cook, and she made a cake. It was as big as—let me see—as big as the moon. It was stuffed with nuts, and raisins, and figs, and candied fruit peel, and over it all was an icing of sugar, thick, and smooth, and very white. And no sooner was the cake home from the baking than the cook put on her bonnet and carried it to the school.

When Henry first saw it, he jumped up and down. He was not patient enough to wait for a knife, but he fell upon the cake tooth and nail. He ate and ate until school began, and after school was over he ate again with his might and main. At night he ate until bedtime, and he put the cake under his bolster when he went to bed and he waked and waked a dozen times that he might take a bite.

But the next day when the dinner bell rang, Henry was not hungry, and was vexed to see how heartily the other children ate. His friends asked him if he would not play at cricket, tan, or kits. Ah! Henry could not; so they played without him, and Henry could scarcely stand upon his legs. He went and sat down in a corner, and the head master sent for the apothecary to come with all his phials of physic. After some days Henry was well again, but his mother said that she would never let him have another cake.

Now there was another scholar in the same school, whose name was Francis. He had written his mother a very pretty letter without one misspelled word or blot, and so his mother, like the mother of Henry, sent him a great cake.

Francis decided that he would not be so unwise as to follow the example of Henry, so he took the cake, which was so heavy that he could hardly lift it, and he watched to see that no one was looking, and he slipped up to his chamber and put the cake in his box under lock and key. Every day at play time he used to slip away from his companions, go upstairs on tiptoe, and cut off a tolerable slice of his cake which he would eat by himself. For a whole week did he keep this up, but alas— the cake was so exceedingly large! At last the cake grew dry, and quickly after it became moldy. Finally the maggots got into it, and Francis, with great reluctance, was obliged to throw it away.

There was a third little gentleman who went to the same school as Henry and Francis, and his name was Gratian. One day his mother, whom he loved very dearly, sent him a cake because she also loved him. No sooner had it arrived than Gratian called his friends all about him, and said:

"Come! Look at what my mother has sent me. You must, each one, have a piece." So the children all got around the cake as bees resort to a flower, just blown, and Gratian divided the cake with a knife into as many pieces as he had invited boys, with one piece over, for himself. His own piece he said he would eat the next day, and he began playing games with the boys.

But a very short time had passed, as they were playing, when a poor man who was carrying a fiddle came into the school yard. He had a very long, gray beard, and he was guided by a little dog who went before him, for the old man was blind.

The children noticed how dexterous was the little dog in leading, and how he shook a bell which hung underneath his collar, as if to say:

"Do not throw down or run against my master!"

When the two had come into the yard, the old man sat down upon a stone, and said:

"My dear little gentlemen, I will play you all the pretty tunes that I know, if you will give me leave."

The children wished for nothing half so much as to hear the music, so the old man put his violin in tune and then played over jigs and tunes that had been new in former times.

But Gratian, who was standing close to him, noticed that while he played his jolliest airs, a tear would often roll down his cheeks. And Gratian asked him why he wept.

"Because," said the old man, "I am hungry. I have not any one in the world to feed me, or my faithful dog."

Then Gratian felt like crying, too, and he ran to fetch the cake which he had saved to eat himself.   He brought it out with joy, and as he ran along he said:

"Here, good man, here is some cake for you."

Then Gratian put the cake into the old man's hands and he, laying down his fiddle, wiped his eyes and began to eat.   At every piece he put into his mouth he gave a bit to his faithful little dog, who ate from his hand; and Gratian, standing by, had as much pleasure as if he had eaten the cake himself.

*From the French of Monsieur Berquin's L'Ami des Enfants—
1784*

STORIES SELECTED BECAUSE OF THEIR SENSE AP-
PEAL TO THE CHILD'S MIND

THE GINGERBREAD BOY
        Sara Cone Bryant, in How to Tell Stories to Children
JOHNNY CAKE   *In Firelight Stories*
THE TWO LITTLE COOKS
            Laura E. Richards, in Five Minute Stories
WHAT WAS HER NAME?
            Laura E. Richards, in Five Minute Stories
THE COOKY   *Laura E. Richards, in The Golden Windows*
THE MOUSE PIE   *Folk Tale*
THE MOUSE AND THE SAUSAGE
            Frances Hodgson Burnett, in St. Nicholas
TINY HARE AND THE ECHO
                Anne Schutze, in Little Animal Stories
WHY THE SEA IS SALT
        Sara Cone Bryant, in How to Tell Stories to Children

FOR THE STORY TELLER

The Proud Little Grain of Wheat
> Frances Hodgson Burnett, in Saint Nicholas

The Story the Milk Told
> Gertrude Hayes Noyce, in In the Child's World

The Pied Piper of Hamelin
> Sara Cone Bryant, in How to Tell Stories to Children

Old Pipes and the Dryad   Frank Stockton, in Fanciful Tales

The Big Red Apple
> Kate Whiting Patch, in For the Children's Hour.

The Christmas Cake   Maud Lindsay, in More Mother Stories

CHAPTER III

WHEN THE CURTAIN RISES

A TIRED-OUT, unenthusiastic school teacher in one of our large public schools was recently endeavoring to secure the attention of her class for a story. This story hour was, for her, just one lap in the march of the day's routine, a period to be finished as soon as possible, and she began it in a stereotyped way.

"I am going to tell you a story, children," she said, "and I want every child in the room to sit up straight, put his feet *flat* on the floor and fold his hands. When everybody is ready, I will begin."

In contrast one is reminded of another teacher, who opened her story hour in a different way. In point of fact, she did not really *open* it at all in the formal understanding of the word. Nor did she have any specified period of the day for telling stories. When her class was fatigued and needed a note of relaxation, when they were restless and needed calming, when they seemed to need inspiration, she gave the signal for books and pencils to be put away and with no further introduction she took the children with her to Story Land for a space, *opening her story in so interesting a way* that she compelled attention without asking for it.

The instance of the first story teller is an example of securing a child's *voluntary attention.*

The second story teller illustrated a method of securing a child's *involuntary,* almost unconscious *attention.*

Especially in the case of the little child who is beginning his school work, and even up to the more mature years of childhood, voluntary attention, *that mental operation in which the will is called upon to open the doors of the senses and let in knowledge,* is almost too much for us to ask of a child. The wonderful machinery of the mind has provided another and much more economic means of knowledge acquisition. *Certain mind stimuli will set the whole wireless system of perception, association and memory going* without any effort on the part of the story teller save that of discovering the stimuli. In other words, we must secure *involuntary attention in children through studying their interests.* The story that opens with *headlines of child interest* as compelling as those of one of our yellow news sheets will hold a child's attention without his being in the least conscious of his attitude of mind toward it. Voluntary attention, the mind attitude toward a story that is brought about by folded hands and straight backs, is very likely to lapse, to develop a will-o'-the-wisp character and finally lose itself. *Concentrated attention can be secured in children only through the medium of appealing to child interest.*

The successful story teller will bear in mind the fact, in selecting stories to tell, that the good story for children of any age, and adults too, for that matter, should have one of the qualities that characterize a successful drama. *It must catch the attention of the audience the moment the curtain rises.* There must be no long explanation, no descriptive scenes and painful dragging in of the plot. Children do not care a rap for the creating of atmosphere. They do not care how long ago the story events happened, or why they happened. What they are eager for is a quick story appeal made the second that the story curtain rolls up.

Each story told to children ought to be selected having in mind its beginning. The story teller must ask herself another set of questions:

"Does the story interest begin with my first paragraph, my first sentence, my first word?"

"Will the opening of my story find an apperceptive basis for attention in the minds of my children?"

"Has my story a sense appeal in the first sentence?"

Any one of these qualities of story opening will help to win the sympathy of the child audience and will find a ready response in involuntary attention.

A class of little street boys waged continued warfare upon one of the New York Settlement

Houses. They broke the windows, mobbed the Settlement children and carefully evaded the police. The Settlement story teller decided, one night, to open the doors of the house to the gang of boys and see if it would not be possible to win them over to an interest in the work of the Settlement and lead them to obey the laws of society through stories. The boys entered the building like a besieging army. They shouted, stamped, stampeded into the room that had been assigned them and throwing down chairs and overturning tables they proceeded to produce a scene of Bedlam. The story teller made no effort to control the boys. She secured for herself a place of vantage in the center of the room. When there was an instant's lull in the uproar that the boys were making, as they took breath for more rowdyism, she said in a low, even tone of voice:

"There was once a little Indian boy who rode fifty miles on the cow-catcher of an engine."

Then she waited and the boys waited, too, breathlessly eager for her next words. When she saw that she had caught the interest of her audience, she proceeded with the story in the same even, low voice, not so much telling the boys a story, apparently, but just *telling a story,* every sentence of which painted a word picture and the whole being a graphic series of moving pictures unrolled on a story film before her audience. She gave the story facts about the Indian lad who had never seen a locomotive and stole a daring ride on one because he thought it was a fire-horse. One by one the boys seated themselves quietly on the chairs or on the floor to listen. Several lay flat upon the floor, crawling stealthily nearer to the story teller as their interest in the story deepened. Throughout the entire telling of the story the room was absolutely still, and when the climax came the boys asked for another story. From that evening they were the Settlement's stanch allies.

It would have been impossible to secure the voluntary attention of these boys. The fact that some one wanted to tell them a story would have probably inspired them to more lawlessness. If the story teller had begun the story after this fashion:—

"Fifty years ago there were few railways in the western part of our country. The prairies were peopled by Comanche tribes who were unfamiliar with the inventions of civilization, and the first train that ran through an Indian settlement inspired an Indian lad to a strange deed"—

Not a boy would have listened. This form of story beginning is *bad* and phenomenally common in many stories for children. It is an example of *words,* not *interest stimuli.* It explains a story situation instead of *presenting* it. A story to secure the involuntary attention of children should have the quality of a crashing orchestral overture, a thunder clap, a pistol shot—so unexpected, compelling, and penetrating will it be.

"There was once a little Indian boy who rode fifty miles on the cow-catcher of an engine!"

Could there be a more stimulating story beginning for a group of boys than this? There is an apperceptive appeal in the Indian lad. He was not a man, not a chieftain, but just a little lad like themselves. There is an immedi-

47

ate sense appeal in the steam-engine image that the story beginning brings to their minds. Smoke, smell, bell ringing, whistle blowing, steam escaping, and the rattle of iron wheels on iron tracks are all recalled to a boy's mind in one glorious bit of imagination whose only stimulus is the word *engine*. Then, to clinch the apperceptive and sensory appeal of the sentence, is the quick introduction of a new story interest—the Indian boy did a deed that they, in their wildest dreams, had never considered—he rode an engine.

If a story, otherwise good, opens poorly—is too wordy, too descriptive, too pedantic—study the story carefully for its main interest and, selecting just the right words to convey this overture of interest, begin *there*. It will be discovered that certain of the classic, favorite tales of childhood fulfill this story test. They open compellingly and carry the interest that was stimulated in the first paragraph clear through to the end.

"There were once five and twenty tin soldiers who were all brothers, for they had been made out of the same old tin spoon."

Hans Christian Andersen used the child's instinctive love of counting his toys, and a bit of humor that tickles a child's fancy, when he wrote this opening paragraph of his wonderful old allegory, "The Faithful Tin Soldier."

"Once upon a time there lived a cat and a parrot and they thought they would ask each other to dinner, turn and turn about."

This folk tale of "The Greedy Cat" opens with a strong sense appeal. The children's interest aroused in the first sentence by means of the progressive dinner arrangement of the famous cat is sustained to the last word of the story.

"He was a wee little duck with a very long tail, so he was called Drakestail. Now Drakestail had some money of his very, very own and the King asked if he might take it. So Drakestail loaned all his money to the King—"

In this old folk tale, the gist of which is the merry adventures of a duck, the story interest begins with the first sentence. The children are introduced, with no unnecessary preliminaries of description or explanation to the hero,

Drakestail, and then they are plunged into the story itself, interesting and direct in its appeal.

"Some children were at play in their playground one day, when a herald rode through the town, blowing a trumpet and crying aloud: 'The King! The King is coming!'"

In this story, Laura E. Richards' "Coming of the King," to be found in her collection of short stories, "The Golden Windows," a strong sense appeal commands the child's involuntary attention at the beginning of the story. The familiar figures, children at play in their playground, are introduced to the sound of a trumpet's call, instantly attracting the attention of the child listeners.

Once the story teller has learned story selection, having in mind a beginning that will hold the attention of her audience from her first word, her success will be secured. It is also possible to carry this interest which has been secured for the child the instant that the curtain rolls up, straight through to the end of the story, because of its compelling beginning. The opening paragraph of a child's story should be the theme, tuned to the key and melody of child interest about which and on which the rest of the story plays. The noteworthy dinner of the cat and the mouse forms the keynote for the rest of the classic adventures of the Greedy Cat. The "wee little duck" and the avaricious old King whom we meet in the first paragraph are the main actors in the story drama of Drakestail. The playground of the children that we see in the first sentence of Mrs. Richards' "The Coming of the King," is the scene of a story miracle almost unparalleled in short story writing for children.

Cutting out unnecessary description, avoiding any explanation as to why you are telling the story, introducing your thunder clap, your trumpet, your story hero in the first sentence —this is the way to begin a story.

"The Prince's Visit," by Horace Scudder, is an excellent example of sustained story interest brought about by means of a compelling story opening.

THE PRINCE'S VISIT

It was a holiday in the city, for the Prince was to arrive. As soon as the cannon should sound, the people might know that the Prince had landed from the steamer, and when they should hear the bells ring that was as much as being told that the Prince, dressed splendidly, and wearing a feather in his cap, was actually on his way up the main street of the city, seated in a carriage drawn by four coal-black horses, and with the soldiers and music going on before.

It was holiday in the workshops, too, and little Job was listening for the cannon and the bells. He was only a poor, foolish little lad, and he did nothing all day long but turn the crank that worked a great washing machine; but when he heard the boom of the guns, he shuffled out and made his way home.

Ever since he had heard of the Prince's coming, Job had dreamed of nothing else. He bought a picture of the Prince and pinned it up on the wall over his bed; and when he came home at night, tired and hungry, he would sit down by his mother, who mended holes in the laundry clothes, and talk about the Prince until he could keep his eyes open no longer; and then his mother would kiss him and send him to bed.

To-day he hurried so fast that he was quite out of breath when he reached the old house where he lived.

"The cannon went off, mother!" he cried. "The Prince is come!"

"Everything is ready, Job," said his mother. "You will find all your things in a row on the bed." And Job tumbled into his room to dress for the holiday. Everything was there as his mother had said; all the old things renewed, and all the new things pieced together that she had worked on so long, and every stitch of which Job had overlooked and almost directed.

"Isn't it splendid?" he said as he looked at himself in a mirror. Round his throat was a white satin scarf that shone in contrast to his dingy coat, and it was pinned with an old brooch which Job treasured as the apple of his eye.

"If you'd only let me wear the feather, mother," he said.

"You look splendidly, Job, and don't need it," said she cheerfully; "and, besides, the Prince wears one, and what would he think if he saw you with one, too?"

"Sure enough," said Job, and then he kissed her and started off.

"I don't believe," he said as he went up the court, "that the Prince would mind my wearing a feather; but mother didn't want me to. Hark, there are the bells! He must have started!"

It was a long way from Job's house to the main street, and he would have to hurry if he were going to see the grand procession. On he shambled, knocking against the flag-stones, and nearly falling down at every step. He was now in a cross street, which would bring him before long to the main street, and he even thought he heard the distant music and the cheers of the crowd.

But just then he stumbled upon something which tripped him. He would have hurried on, but he heard a cry, and a groan of pain. He looked back, and he saw what he had stumbled over. It was a poor beggar boy, without home or friends, dirty and unsightly enough, and clad in ragged clothing, and he was lying on the sidewalk, too ill to move. As Job turned, the boy looked up at him and stretched out his hands, but he was too weak to speak.

"He is sick!" said Job. "Hilloa!" but every one was intent upon the procession, and no one heard him.

"The Prince is coming," he said; and he

turned as if to run. But the beggar would not away from his eyes.

"He is sick," said Job again, bending down, "I will take him home to mother."

"Hurrah! Hurrah! There he is! The Prince! The Prince!"

In the carriage drawn by four coal-black horses rode the Prince; and he was dressed in splendid clothes and he wore a feather in his cap.

Job wiped the tears from his eyes as he heard the music and the cheering so far away, but he lifted the little beggar boy in his arms—and started for home.

And as he passed along the street with his burden, he heard a sound of beautiful music as if all the angels were singing together, and he looked up into the blue sky above the chimneys and roofs of the city, and he saw the angels with the Prince in the midst of them moving by, and they were all smiling on him, poor, simple Job.

So Job saw the Prince pass, too.

HORACE E. SCUDDER.

From "Dream Children." Used by special permission of Houghton, Mifflin Company.

LIST OF STORIES IN WHICH THE STORY INTEREST IS
TO BE FOUND IN THE FIRST PARAGRAPH

THE FAITHFUL TIN SOLDIER   *Hans Christian Andersen*
THE GREEDY CAT
       Sara Cone Bryant, in How to Tell Stories to Children
HOW DRAKESTAIL WENT TO THE KING   *In Firelight Stories*
THE COMING OF THE KING
       Laura E. Richards, in The Golden Windows
WHY THE MORNING GLORY CLIMBS
       Sara Cone Bryant, in How to Tell Stories to Children
PETER RABBIT   *Beatrix Potter*
THE LITTLE JACKALS AND THE LION
       Sara Cone Bryant, in Stories to Tell to Children
LITTLE HALF CHICK
       Sara Cone Bryant, in Stories to Tell to Children
THE SNOW MAN   *Hans Christian Andersen*
THE BABY QUEEN
       Annie Hamilton Donnell, in For the Children's Hour
MR. FROG AND MR. ELEPHANT   *In Firelight Stories*
THE THREE BILLY GOATS GRUFF   *In Firelight Stories*
BRE'R RABBIT AND THE LITTLE TAR BABY
       Joel Chandler Harris, in Nights with Uncle Remus

CHAPTER IV

USING SUSPENSE TO DEVELOP CONCENTRATION

BECAUSE we have discovered that a story is able to do much for a child; make him feel comfortable and at home in a new environment because it brings to his mind so compellingly the well-known and loved surroundings of some former environment, stimulate his senses to added activity, and secure his involuntary attention, we are going one step farther. We will make a fresh discovery. We will find a story quality that will develop sustained attention in children; will give them the power to concentrate. Not only will our story open with such a clarion note of interest that it will compel involuntary attention but after this overture, this *crash* of interest, the perfect child's story will swing into a different sort of construction that will hold the attention secured by its previous yellow headlines of interest.

One story quality more than any other develops this sustained interest on the part of the children who are listening to it — the *quality of suspense.*

What is suspense?

It is so necessary a story quality that it seems to explain itself. Suspense means, *making the children wait for the rest of the story.* It means that *the different scenes, the events that go to make up the story, are told in the order of their relative interest appeal to the child mind.* The child listens, attends involuntarily as the story proceeds because *he wants to know what is coming next.* Each scene of the story is unfinished for him; he must wait for a fulfillment of what he expects, looks for, longs for in the story. One sentence, one paragraph makes him *curious* to hear the following one. The story structure is like a child's stringing of beads. Upon a white thread of interest the colored glass balls which go to make up the whole circlet of the story plot are strung, as a child would pick them out, each inadequate

58

and incomplete without its component—one bead slipped down to make a place for the next one.

Suspense is the story quality that stimulates curiosity and in this way develops concentrated thinking on the part of the child.

Certain old folk stories have the quality of suspense developed to a high degree and through their accumulative, *building on* character of construction compel every child's attention. It is wise to look for this quality in selecting stories to tell to the very young child whose ability to attend for any length of time is undeveloped. Through the involuntary, sustained interest he develops, through listening to the story he becomes able to fix his attention upon other human affairs. An old nursery tale of New England, reported by Clifton Johnson, illustrates with unusual vividness the use of suspense in sustaining a story interest that holds the attention of any child up to the last word of the story.

THE TRAVELS OF A FOX

A fox was digging behind a stump, and he found a bumble-bee. The fox put the bumble-bee in a bag and he traveled.

The first house he came to he went in, and he said to the mistress of the house:

"May I leave my bag here while I go to Squintum's?"

"Yes," said the woman.

"Then be careful not to open the bag," said the fox.

But as soon as the fox was out of sight, the woman just took a little peep into the bag and out flew the bumble-bee, and the rooster caught him and ate him up.

After a while the fox came back. He took up his bag and he saw that the bumble-bee was gone, and he said to the woman:

"Where is my bumble-bee?"

And the woman said:

"I just untied the bag, and the bumble-bee flew out, and the rooster ate him up."

"Very well," said the fox, "I must have the rooster, then."

So he caught the rooster and put him in his bag, and traveled.

And the next house he came to he went in, and said to the mistress of the house:

"May I leave my bag here while I go to Squintum's?"

"Yes," said the woman.

"Then be careful not to open the bag," said the fox.

But as soon as the fox was out of sight, the woman just took a little peep into the bag, and the rooster flew out, and the pig caught him and ate him up.

After a while the fox came back, and he took up his bag and he saw that the rooster was not in it, and he said to the woman: "Where is my rooster?"

And the woman said:

"I just untied the bag, and the rooster flew out, and the pig ate him."

"Very well," said the fox, "I must have the pig, then."

So he caught the pig and put him in his bag, and traveled.

And the next house he came to he went in, and he said to the mistress of the house:

"May I leave my bag here while I go to Squintum's?"

"Yes," said the woman.

"Then be careful not to open the bag," said the fox.

But as soon as the fox was out of sight, the woman just took a little peep into the bag, and the pig jumped out, and the ox ate him.

After a while the fox came back. He took up his bag and he saw that the pig was gone, and he said to the woman:

"Where is my pig?"

And the woman said:

"I just untied the bag, and the pig jumped out, and the ox ate him."

"Very well," said the fox, "I must have the ox, then."

So he caught the ox and put him in his bag, and traveled.

And the next house he came to he went in, and he said to the mistress of the house:

"May I leave my bag here while I go to Squintum's?"

"Yes," said the woman.

"Then be careful not to open the bag," said the fox.

But as soon as the fox was out of sight, the woman just took a little peep into the bag, and the ox got out, and the woman's little boy chased him away off over the fields.

After a while the fox came back. He took up his bag, and he saw that the ox was gone, and he said to the woman:

"Where is my ox?"

And the woman said:

"I just untied the string, and the ox got out, and my little boy chased him away off over the fields."

"Very well," said the fox, "I must have the little boy, then."

So he caught the little boy and he put him in his bag, and he traveled.

And the next house he came to he went in, and he said to the mistress of the house:

"May I leave my bag here while I go to Squintum's?"

"Yes," said the woman.

"Then be careful not to open the bag," said the fox.

The woman was making cake, and her children were around her asking for some.

"Oh, mother, give me a piece," said one; and, "Oh, mother, give me a piece," said the others.

And the smell of the cake came to the little boy who was weeping and crying in the bag, and he heard the children asking for cake and he said: "Oh, mammy, give me a piece."

Then the woman opened the bag and took the little boy out, and she put the house-dog in the bag in the little boy's place. And the little boy stopped crying and had some cake with the others.

After a while the fox came back. He took up his bag and he saw that it was tied fast, and he put it over his back and traveled far into the deep woods. Then he sat down and untied the bag, and if the little boy had been there in the bag things would have gone badly with him.

But the little boy was safe in the woman's house, and when the fox untied the bag the house-dog jumped out and ate him all up.

An old nursery tale of New England. Reprinted by permission of Clifton Johnson.

The point of interest for children in this story lies in their wonder as to what is going to happen next. It begins with a note of the unusual.

"How strange for a fox to put a bumble bee in a bag," the children say. "Will the next sentence tell us why he did it?"

Then a number of questions present themselves to the child mind.

"Will the woman untie the bag?"

"Will the person at *this* house do the same thing?"

"Is it possible that *every* woman will open the bag?"

Another series of questions confronts the child.

"What manner of beast will the fox take at *this* house and put in his bag?"

And so the suspense is sustained until the children's curiosity is satisfied at the end of the story. Not alone has the story been a bit of mental gymnastics for the child, it has given him added mental power in the listening. Above and behind the mental process of waiting to see what unusual and unexpected scene of the story drama will be presented to him next, *he has been exercising his will in concentrating upon the process of waiting.* His power of sustained attention has been strengthened materially and ineffaceably.

For the very young child, the suspensive element in story telling must be very simple. It will consist often in *repetition,* the pleasureable recurrence in the story of certain *sounds* that the child likes and is willing to wait for —sort of half way houses on the story road they are, where his mind wheels may stop and rest awhile—sign posts that lead the way to the end of the road. Sometimes this story suspense for the little folks is brought about through a jingle introduced into the story and repeated with certain changes as in the old folk tale of "The Cat and the Mouse." Again suspense is brought about by means of a change of intonation on the part of the story teller. She adapts her voice to the needs of the story as in "The Three Bears" to the inexpressible delight of the children. This is a primitive sort of suspense quality to be found in the most elemental stories for children but it has its important place in the discipline of the child mind. The little child's first attempts to attend have a butterfly quality. His mind flies from one stimulus to another with no very long stop anywhere. This is as it should be, for the world of sensations in which the child is plunged as an *ego* is a varied, crowded world and there is temptation offered him to sip each flower, smell each new odor, touch everything and see everything with which he comes in contact. But a suspensive story holds him to one related set of images for a brief space and through this concentration, however simple it may be, he is developing the power of willed attention.

As children grow older, the suspense quality for which we must look in their stories will not consist in *repetition of sounds, jingles and phrases,* but in their *sequence of events leading toward some unknown climax.* This is a more difficult and subtle form of suspense to secure. Here, the beads are strung upon their thread, not in groups of white interspersed with occasional red ones, but rather in the order of the rainbow in bands of color that complement and complete each other. Any description of this more highly developed suspensive story would be absolutely inadequate, for the quality has to be *felt* by the story teller first and then *felt for* by her.

An adapted version of the story of the first meeting of John Ridd and Lorna Doone taken from the novel, "Lorna Doone," gives an illuminating exemplification of the kind of suspense that holds a child breathless, *waiting for the unknown something that is to follow.* The story teller should endeavor to discover and introduce some suspense, either elemental, as in the case of the folk tale, or of the more elusive quality, illustrated in this story, into all her stories.

LITTLE LORNA DOONE

Almost everybody knows how pleasant and soft the fall of land is round about Plover's Barrows Farm. There are trees and bright green grass and orchards full of contentment, and you can scarce espy the brook, although you hear it everywhere. But it is there, where the valley bends and the stream goes along with it, and pretty meadows slope their breast, and the sun spreads on the water. And nearly all the land until you come to Nicholas Snow's belonged to the Ridd farm—to little John Ridd's father.

John's mother had long been ailing and not well able to eat much. Now John chanced to remember that once at the time of the holidays he had brought his dear mother from Tiverton a jar of pickled loaches; and she had said that in all her life she had never tasted anything fit to be compared with them.

So, one St. Valentine's Day, in the forenoon, without saying a word to any one, John started away to get some loaches for his mother just to make her eat a bit.

It was a bitter cold day, but John doffed his shoes and hose and put them in a bag about his neck, and left his little coat at home that he might walk better. When he had traveled two miles or so he found a good stream flowing softly into the body of the brook. The water was freezing, and John's toes were aching, and he drew up on the bank and rubbed them well with a sprout of young sting-nettle, and having skipped about a little was inclined to eat a bit. As he ate, his spirits rose, so he put the bag round his neck again and buckled his breeches far up from the knee, and crossing the brook, went stoutly up under the branches which hung so dark on the Bagworthy River.

The day was falling fast behind the brown of the hilltops, and the trees seemed giants ready to beat the boy. And every moment as the sky was clearing up for a white frost, the cold of the water underfoot on the fells got worse and worse, until John was fit to cry with it. And so, in a sorry plight, he came to an opening in the bushes where a great black pool lay in front, whitened at the sides with foam froth.

The boy shuddered, and drew back, not at the pool itself, but at the whirling manner and wisping of white threads upon it in circles, round and round; and the center, black as jet. He did not stop to look much for fear, though, but crawled along over the fork of rocks where the water had scooped the stone out, and shunning the ledge from whence it rose like the mane of a white horse into the broad black pool, softly he let his feet slip into the dip and rush of the torrent.

But John had reckoned without his host, for the green waves came down like great bottles upon him, and his legs were gone from under him in a minute. He was borne up upon a rock, and he won a footing, but there was no choice left except to climb somehow up that hill of water or else be washed down into the pool and whirl around until it drowned him, for there was no chance of going back by the way he had come down. So John started carefully, step by step, stopping to hold on by the cliff when he found a resting place, and pant a while. But the greatest danger came when he saw no jeopardy, but ran up a patch of black ooze weed which stuck out in a boastful manner not far from the summit. Here he fell, and was like to have broken his knee cap, but his elbow caught in a hole in the rock and so he managed to start again.

But the little boy was in a most dreadful fright now, and at last the rush of water drove him back again into the middle. Then he made up his mind to die at last; only it did seem such a pity after fighting so long, to give in. The light was coming upon him, and again he fought toward it, when suddenly he felt fresh air, and fell into it headlong.

When John came to himself, his hands were full of young grass and mold, and a little girl was kneeling at his side and rubbing his forehead tenderly.

"I am so glad," she whispered softly, as John opened his eyes and looked at her. "Now you will try to be better, won't you?"

The little boy had never heard so sweet a sound as came from between her red lips while she knelt and gazed at him; nor had he ever seen anything so beautiful as the large dark eyes, full of pity and wonder. His eyes wandered down the black shower of her hair; and where it fell on the turf, among it, like an early star, was the first primrose of the season.

"What is your name?" she said, "and how did you come here? Oh, how your feet are bleeding! I must tie them up for you. And no shoes or stockings! Is your mother very poor, boy?"

"No," said John, a little vexed. "We are rich enough to buy all this great meadow if we choose. Here are my shoes and stockings."

"Why, they are quite as wet as your feet. Oh, please let me manage them. I will do it very softly."

"Oh, I don't mind that," said John, "but how you are looking at me. I never saw any one like you before. My name is John Ridd. What is your name?"

"Lorna Doone," she answered in a low voice as if afraid of it, and hanging her head so he could see only her forehead and eyelashes; "if you please, my name is Lorna Doone, and I thought you must have known it," and her blushes turned to tears and her tears to long, low sobs.

"Don't cry," said John, "whatever you do. I will give you all my fish, Lorna, and catch some more for my mother; only don't be angry with me."

Young and harmless as she was, her name alone made guilt of her; yet there was John, a yeoman's son, and there was she, a little lady born. Though her hair had fallen down, and some of her frock was touched with wet, behold, her dress was pretty enough for the queen of all the angels. All from her waist to her neck was white, plaited in close like a curtain, and the dark soft tresses of her hair, and the shadowy light of her eyes made it seem yet whiter.

"John," she said, "why did you ever come here? Do you know what the robbers would do to us if they found you here with me?"

"Beat us, I dare say," said John, "or me at least. They could never beat you."

"No, they would kill us both, and bury us here by the water because you have found your way up here. Now please go; oh, please go!"

"I never saw any one like you, Lorna, and I must come back again to-morrow, and so must you. I will bring you such lots of things—there are apples still—and I caught a thrush—and I will bring you the loveliest dog—"

"Hush!"

A shout came down the valley, and Lorna's face was full of terror.

"Do you see that hole?" she cried.

It was a niche in the rock which skirted the meadow. In the fading twilight John could just see it.

"Look! Look!" She could hardly speak from

73

terror. "There is a way out from the top of it; they would kill me if I told of it. Oh, here they come; I can see them!"

The little maid turned white as the snow which hung on the rocks above her, and she looked at the water and then at John. She began to sob aloud, but John drew her behind the bushes and close down to the water. Crouching in that hollow nest they saw a dozen fierce men come down on the other side of the water.

"Queen! Queen!" they were shouting here and there, and now and then. "Where is our little queen gone?"

"They always call me 'queen,' and I shall have to be their queen by and by," Lorna whispered. "Oh, they are crossing, and they are sure to see us."

"I must get down into the water," said John, "and you must go to sleep."

She saw in a moment how to do it, and there was no time to lose.

"Now mind you, never come again," she whispered over her shoulder as she crept away, "only I shall come sometimes."

John crept into the water and lay down with his head between two blocks of stone, and all this time the robbers were shouting so that all the rocks round the valley rang. The boy was desperate between fear and wretchedness till he caught sight of the little maid, but he knew that for her sake he must be brave and hide himself.

Lorna was lying beneath a rock not far away, feigning to be fast asleep. Presently one of the robbers came upon her, and he stopped and gazed awhile at her fairness and innocence. Then he caught her up in his arms and kissed her.

"Here our queen is! Here's the captain's daughter," he shouted, "fast asleep."

He set her dainty little form upon his great square shoulder, and her narrow feet in one broad hand; and so he marched away with the purple velvet of her skirt ruffling his long black beard, and the silken length of her hair fetched out, like a cloud of the wind behind her.

John crept into a bush for warmth, and then, as daylight sank beneath the forget-me-not of stars, he knew that it was time to get away, and he managed to crawl from the bank to the niche in the cliff that Lorna had shown him. How he climbed up, and crossed the clearing, and found his way home across the Bagworthy forest was more than he could remember afterward, because of his weariness.

All the supper was in, and the men sitting at

the white table with Annie and Lizzie near by—
and all were eager to begin, save only the mother.
John was of a mind to stay out in the dark by the
woodstack, being so late, but the way his mother
was looking out of the doorway got the better of
him, so he went inside and ate his supper, and
held his tongue as to where he had been all day
and evening. But if he had been of a mind he
could have told them many things.

RICHARD D. BLACKMORE.

Adapted.

LITTLE IN-A-MINUTE

ILLUSTRATING STORY SUSPENSE WHICH APPEALS
TO YOUNGEST CHILDREN

The big, yellow Sun smiled down upon them
and the Singing Brook hummed pretty little tunes
for them to listen to. They were two little boys
at play with a whole, long beautiful day ahead.

They looked almost exactly alike, did these two
little boys. Bobby wore a wide-brimmed sun hat
with a blue band around it, and Dicky wore a wide-
brimmed sun hat with a red band around it.
Bobby wore a brown linen sailor suit with blue
anchors on the collar and Dicky wore a brown linen
sailor suit with red anchors on the collar. Bobby

had a beautiful toy ship to play with, and Dicky had a beautiful ship, too. As for the ships, *they* looked *just* exactly alike. Each beautiful toy ship was painted white and green, and each had a big white sail as wide and pretty as a dove's wing, and each had a strong little rudder painted red.

Bobby and Dicky had made a make-believe wharf in the Singing Brook of sticks and stones and nice black mud. There, anchored at the wharf, lay the two beautiful toy boats, their white sails flapping and fat with wind. When their strings were loosed from the wharf, the Whispering Wind would carry the two little boats way, way down the Singing Brook to another little make-believe wharf made of sticks and stones and nice black mud that Bobby and Dicky had made farther on.

So the Sun smiled down more happily and the Singing Brook sang a merrier tune than the last one and Bobby and Dicky began to play.

"I am going to load my boat with little green apples, Dicky," said Bobby. "Perhaps the Old Chipmunk who lives at the foot of the Pine Tree will go aboard and unload them."

Bobby began gathering small green apples as fast as he could and putting them on the deck of his little ship, but Dicky sat on the bank of the Singing Brook, doing nothing and only watching.

"When are you going to load your ship, Dicky?" Bobby asked as he put in the last apples.

"In a minute," Dicky answered, but before the minute had gone, Bobby's ship, its white sail flying, had started down the Singing Brook to the other wharf. Dicky jumped up and loosed his boat from its moorings, but it was very far behind Bobby's all the way. The two little boys hurried softly between the willow trees that stood along the edge of the Singing Brook. As they came to the other make-believe wharf they saw the Old Chipmunk creep out of his house at the foot of the Pine Tree and go out on the wharf to wait for the little ship to come in. When it came, he unloaded all the cargo of apples and carried them over to his cellar. But when Dicky's ship came in, so late and so empty, the Old Chipmunk did nothing but smell of it. Then he sat on the end of the make-believe wharf in the sunshine and basked and did not even look at Dicky's ship again.

"I have thought of something very nice to do, now," said Bobby as the two little boys carried their ships back again. "We will play that the flowers are children and we will give them a ride in our ships."

78

"Yes, we will!" agreed Dicky.

So Bobby picked many little flower children; clovers in pink bonnets and buttercups in wide yellow hats and daisies in gold bonnets with white strings, and he put them all carefully aboard his ship. But Dicky only stood by in the grass and watched.

"When are you going to fill your boat with flowers, Dicky?" Bobby asked as he helped the last flower child aboard.

"In a minute," Dicky answered, but just then down the Singing Brook came the Whispering Wind. It filled the little white sails and away sailed the two little ships, the flower children aboard Bobby's fluttering and dancing with the joy of having a boat ride.

The two little boys raced along the bank to watch and they saw a wonderful thing happen. All the way down the Singing Brook, pretty passengers joined the flower children on board Bobby's ship. A gold butterfly fluttered down to the deck with his yellow and black wings, kissing the clovers beneath their pink bonnets. A shiny black bumble bee tumbled down to the deck with his gold, gossamer wings and began to drone summer stories to the buttercups. A silver dragon fly darted down to the ship with his rainbow tinted wings to mend

79

the white strings of the daisies' caps which had been torn by the frolicsome Whispering Wind. When Bobby's ship reached the other wharf it looked like an excursion boat, but, ah, Dicky's ship was quite empty. There had been no flower children on board to call the butterflies, the bumble bees and the dragon flies.

"I know the nicest play of all, now," said Bobby after he had helped the flower children from his ship and put their feet in the Singing Brook that they might wade there all the rest of the day and keep cool and fresh and sweet.

"We will take our ships back, Dicky, and have a race."

"Oh, that will be nice!" Dicky answered, so the two little boys carried the two ships back and launched them, side by side, in the Singing Brook.

"One—two—" began Bobby, but before he said *three* he heard their mother's voice floating over the fields and as far as their playground.

"Bobby, Dicky, come home," their mother called. "Come home, boys, dinner is ready."

"I'm coming, mother," Bobby called back, putting his hand to his mouth to make a horn. Then he turned to Dicky who still bent low over the bank of the Singing Brook and still held in his hand the string that was tied to the rudder of his ship.

"In a minute," Dicky answered. Bobby ran off over the fields, and soon he was out of sight. He knew that there were fat white potatoes and yellow chicken meat and red cherry dumplings for dinner. Now they were hot, but they would be cold if he did not hurry.

Down by the Singing Brook Dicky waited to launch his ship once more. The Whispering Wind filled the sail a third time, and away sailed the beautiful little toy ship, so pretty with its green and white paint, and its rudder that was painted red. Dicky ran along beside it, to see how fast it sailed. Faster and faster sailed Dicky's ship. It did not stop when it came to the Pine Tree where the Old Chipmunk was busy in his cellar sorting out his apples. It did not stop when it came to the Wading Pool where all the flower children stood, keeping cool and fresh and sweet. On and on sailed the little ship, for the Whispering Wind was taking it a long, long way off to the place where the Singing Brook loses itself in the River and the River goes on down to the Sea.

"Come back. Oh, do come back!" called Dicky to the little ship, but the ship only sailed the faster.

"*Please* come back!" cried Dicky as his beautiful ship sailed out of sight.

In a minute, the Whispering Wind called back. But the little ship never came back.

So Dicky went slowly across the field and home to dinner, but when he reached home what do you think had happened?

The fat, white potatoes, the yellow chicken meat and the red cherry dumplings were *cold*.

CAROLYN SHERWIN BAILEY.

STORIES SELECTED BECAUSE OF THEIR SUSPENSIVE
QUALITY

THE TEENY TINY LADY   *In Firelight Stories*
THE HOBYAHS   *In Firelight Stories*
CHICKEN LITTLE   *In Firelight Stories*
THE LITTLE BOY WHO FOUND HIS FORTUNE   *In Firelight Stories*
THE LITTLE PINK ROSE
        Sara Cone Bryant, in Best Stories to Tell to Children
LITTLE JACK ROLLAROUND
        Sara Cone Bryant, in Best Stories to Tell to Children
LITTLE BLACK SAMBO   *Helen Bannerman*
THE HARE AND THE HEDGEHOG   *Æsop's Fables*
THE GRADUAL FAIRY   *Alice Brown, in The One-Footed Fairy*
HOW JOHNNY CHUCK FOUND THE BEST THING IN THE WORLD
        Thornton Burgess, in Old Mother West Wind

CHAPTER V

STORY CLIMAX

WE have found it helpful to liken the effect that a well-written, well-told story has upon a child's mind to the appeal that a successful drama makes to an audience. We have discovered that the opening paragraph, the first sentence of a child's story should have the quality that characterizes the scene disclosed on the stage when the curtain rolls up— *compelling interest.* Following this curtain raising of the story, there should be a series of pictorial scenes that carry the events that go to make up the story plot, strung upon a slender thread of curiosity, and giving the element of suspense to the story.

Following out this story structure we come, eventually, to the end. The curtain must fall at last before the eyes of the child audience and the closing of the story drama should be as mind stimulating as was its beginning. This is brought about by studying carefully the story climax.

The climax of a story should be a complete surprise to the listener and to the characters in the story, as well.

This quick note of the unexpected coming with compelling suddenness at the end of our story clinches the interest of the plot and makes the story indelible on the child's mind sheet.

Certain well-known instances of climax as exemplified in child stories will clarify for us its *surprise* quality.

In one of the older plantation folk tales, Mr. Elephant and Mr. Frog are pictured as being good friends until Mr. Hare taunts them with their dissimilarity in size and says that Mr. Frog has boasted of the fact that Mr. Elephant is his "riding horse." Then the story continues:

"Mr. Fox and Mr. Tiger and Mr. Lion all followed after Mr. Hare, crying: 'Oho, oho, Mr. Elephant is little Mr. Frog's riding horse.'

"Then Mr. Elephant turned around and he said in a very gruff voice to Mr. Frog:

" 'Did you tell them, grandson, that I was your horse?'

"And Mr. Frog said in a high, squeaky voice:—

" 'No, no, grandfather.'

"But all the time Mr. Frog was thinking of a trick to play on Mr. Elephant.

"The next day, Mr. Elephant and Mr. Frog started off for a long walk.   Mr. Frog had heard of a place where the swamps were deep and muddy. Mr. Elephant knew a place where the bananas grew ripe and thick.   And they spent a pleasant day.   On the way home Mr. Frog hopped up close to Mr. Elephant, and he said in his high, squeaky voice:—

" 'Grandfather, I have no strength to walk. Let me get up on your back.'

" 'Climb up, my grandson,' said Mr. Elephant.

"He put his trunk down for a ladder, and Mr. Frog climbed up.   They had not gone very far when Mr. Frog hopped up close to Mr. Elephant's ear, and he said:—

" 'I am going to fall, grandfather.   Give me some small cords from the roadside that I may bind your mouth, and hold myself upon your back.'

" 'I will, grandson,' said Mr. Elephant.

"So Mr. Elephant stripped some small cords from a birch tree by the roadside, and handed them to Mr. Frog. Then Mr. Frog bound Mr. Elephant's mouth, and they went on a little farther. It was not long, though, before Mr. Frog spoke again to Mr. Elephant.

" 'Grandfather,' he said, 'find me a small green twig that I may fan the mosquitoes from your ears.'

" 'I will, grandson,' said Mr. Elephant, so he broke a small, green twig from the birch tree, and reached it up to Mr. Frog; and just then they came toward home.

" 'See Mr. Elephant,' cried Mr. Hare.

" 'See Mr. Elephant,' cried Mr. Tiger.

" 'See Mr. Elephant,' cried Mr. Lion, and all the others, 'Mr. Elephant is Mr. Frog's horse.'

"Mr. Elephant turned himself about, and he saw Mr. Frog on his back, holding the reins and the whip.

" 'Why, so I am, grandson,' said Mr. Elephant.

"Then Mr. Frog jumped down to the ground, and he laughed and he laughed until he nearly split his coat, because he had played a trick on Mr. Elephant."

86

This quotation serves very well to illustrate perfect story climax. In the beginning of the story, an apparently impossible situation was suggested. To the child listener it seems incredible that an elephant could so far forget his dignity as to serve as the steed of a frog. To the elephant himself, as well, this situation appears to be incompatible with his social status in the jungle. As the story advances, each scene prepares a way for the unexpected *dénouement* and the climax is found in the surprise to the hearers and to Mr. Elephant as well when the curtain falls upon him unwittingly playing the part of "riding horse" to little Mr. Frog.

Hans Christian Andersen's inimitable allegory of "The Ugly Duckling" owes a measure, at least, of its popularity to its perfect climax. In the beautiful word pictures of the story we follow its hero, the Ugly Duckling, through his series of perilous and sorrowful adventures, sympathizing with but not anticipating the outcome of them. In no single one of the scenes of the story do we have a hint of the glorious ending of the hero's journeying. Finally comes a quick, artistic curtain falling:

—"Then he flew toward the beautiful swans. As soon as they saw him they rushed to meet him with outstretched wings.

" 'Kill me!' said the Ugly Duckling; but as he bent his head, what did he see reflected in the water? It was his own image—not a dark, gray bird, ugly to see—but a graceful swan.

"Then the great swans swam around him and stroked his neck with their beaks for a welcome. Some little children came into the garden.

" 'See,' they cried, clapping their hands.

" 'A new swan has come and he is more beautiful than the others!' "—

This story climax is perfect, also, because it carries the element of surprise to the story hearers and the story hero, the Ugly Duckling, as well.

It seems to be almost impossible to find many instances of well constructed climax in the short story for children. The story teller must look for climax and in the event of not being able to find it in the story that she selects for telling, it will be necessary for her to make over her story ending that it may be a complete surprise to her listeners, in this way strengthening the plot greatly. Many stories just *stop,* giving one a feeling of dissatisfaction. There has been no climax to make of the whole a finished picture, complete in its minutest detail of light and shade and forming an unerasable vignette, on the child's mind.

Climax knots the thread of the narrative.

Certain child stories, however, stand out as illuminating instances of what climax means in deepening the mental appeal for the child, *etching* the story picture, so to speak. Nathaniel Hawthorne's "Great Stone Face," forms one instance. A careful reading of the story will disclose Hawthorne's subtle use of suspense, the art of "making his audience wait" for his *dénouement.* He makes us see the fertile valley beneath the great mountain upon whose side there had been sculptured by Nature, the wonderful stone face. We are carried, breathlessly, along upon the tide of the narrative through the boy Ernest's longing to bear the image of these beautiful features, the futile attempts of old Gathergold, old Blood-and-Thunder and the others to prove their likeness to the Great Stone Face until we reach our climax in Ernest's own transformation into the great likeness unsuspected by himself or by us.

It seems to be the great short story writers, only, who have given us really illuminating instances of climax—surprise ending—in stories that will appeal to children in a stimulating way. In Hawthorne's "Snow Image" the curtain falls upon a *surprise* situation. Oscar Wilde leaves us unconsolable at his apparent ending of "The Happy Prince." The little swallow is dead and the Prince has given away his gold and jewels.

"So they pulled down the statue of the Happy Prince who was no longer beautiful and so no longer useful and they melted the statue in the furnace.

" 'What a strange thing!' said the overseer of the workmen at the foundry. 'This broken lead heart will not melt in the furnace. We must throw it away!'

"So they threw it on a dust-heap where the dead swallow was also lying."

But as we hold our breath, the climax is flung gloriously out.

" 'Bring me the two most precious things in the City,' said God to one of His Angels and the Angel brought him the leaden heart and the dead bird.

" 'You have rightly chosen,' said God, 'for in my garden of Paradise this little bird shall sing for evermore, and in my city of gold the Happy Prince shall praise me.' "

In the story of Cosette and her doll in "Les Misérables," Victor Hugo has given us a complete story vignette with a perfectly developed climax of surprise as Jean Valjean gives to Cosette, the "toad" of Madame Thenardier's Kitchen, the doll about which she had dreamed. Laura Richard's short stories for children abound in instances of illuminating climax—no hint of the story ending being given until the curtain falls. Her story of "The Golden Windows" in which a little boy sets out upon a journey to find the windows of gold that he sees beyond the village from his own poor little home and discovers at the end of the day that his own home windows, viewed from a distance are gold and those he has found are gray and dull, is an example of Mrs. Richards' skilled use of climax to force her story point into the child's mind.

The mental appeal of climax is a very real and vital one for the consideration of the story teller. Once we fix in our minds the two characteristics of artistic story ending, *surprise to the story characters and to the children, and an ending that ties the knot of the narrative,* our story curtain will fall, leaving the children a lap farther along in their mental development than they were when the curtain rose.

Old Man Rabbit's Thanksgiving Dinner

ILLUSTRATING STORY CLIMAX WHICH APPEALS TO YOUNGEST CHILDREN

Old Man Rabbit sat at the door of his little house eating a nice, ripe, juicy turnip. It was a cold, frosty day, but Old Man Rabbit was all wrapped up, round and round and round, with yards and yards and yards of his best red wool muffler so he didn't care if the wind whistled through his whiskers and blew his ears up straight. Old Man Rabbit had been exercising, too, and that was another reason why he was so nice and warm.

Early in the morning he had started off, lippity, clippity down the little brown path that lay in front of his house and led to Farmer Dwyer's corn patch. The path was all covered with shiny red leaves. Old Man Rabbit scuffled through them and he carried a great big bag over his back. In the corn patch he found two or three fat, red ears of corn that Farmer Dwyer had missed so he dropped them into his bag. A little farther along he found some purple turnips and some yellow carrots and quite a few russet apples that Farmer Dwyer had arranged in little piles in the orchard. Old Man Rabbit went in the barn, squeezing under the big front door by making himself very flat, and he filled all the chinks in his bag with potatoes and he took a couple of eggs in his paws, for he thought that he might want to stir up a little pudding for himself before the day was over.

Then Old Man Rabbit started off home again down the little brown path, his mouth watering every time his bag bumped against his back and not meeting any one on the way because it was so very, very early in the morning. When he came to his little house he emptied his bag and arranged all his harvest in piles in his front room; the corn in one pile, and the carrots in one pile, the turnips in another pile, and the apples and potatoes in the last pile. He beat up his eggs and stirred some flour with them and filled it full of currants to make a pudding. And when he had put his pudding in a bag and set it boiling on the stove, he went outside to sit awhile and eat a turnip, thinking all the time what a mighty fine old rabbit he was and so clever, too.

Well, while Old Man Rabbit was sitting there in front of his little house, wrapped up in his red muffler and munching the turnip, he heard a little noise in the leaves. It was Billy Chipmunk traveling home to the stone wall where he lived. He was hurrying and blowing on his paws to keep them warm.

"Good morning, Billy Chipmunk," said Old Man Rabbit. "Why are you running so fast?"

"Because I am cold, and I am hungry," answered Billy Chipmunk. "It's going to be a hard winter, a very hard winter—no apples left. I've been looking all the morning for an apple and I couldn't find one."

And with that, Billy Chipmunk went chattering by, his fur standing out straight in the wind.

No sooner had he passed than Old Man Rabbit saw Molly Mouse creeping along through the little brown path, her long gray tail rustling the red leaves as she went.

"Good morning, Molly Mouse," said Old Man Rabbit.

"Good morning," answered Molly Mouse in a wee little voice.

"You look a little unhappy," said Old Man Rabbit, taking another bite of his turnip.

"I have been looking and looking for an ear of corn," said Molly Mouse in a sad little chirping voice. "But the corn has all been harvested. It's going to be a very hard winter, a very hard winter."

And Molly Mouse trotted by out of sight.

Pretty soon, Old Man Rabbit heard somebody else coming along by his house. This time it was Tommy Chickadee hopping by and making a great to-do, chattering and scolding as he came.

"Good morning, Tommy Chickadee," said Old Man Rabbit.

But Tommy Chickadee was too much put out about something to remember his manners. He just chirped and scolded, because he was cold and he couldn't find a single crumb or a berry or anything at all to eat. Then he flew away, his

95

feathers puffed out with the cold until he looked like a little round ball, and all the way he chattered and scolded more and more.

Old Man Rabbit finished his turnip, eating every single bit of it, even to the leaves. Then he went in his house to poke the fire in his stove and to see how the pudding was cooking. It was doing very well indeed, bumping against the pot as it bubbled and boiled, and smelling very fine indeed. Old Man Rabbit looked around his house at the corn and the carrots and the turnips and the apples and the potatoes and then he had an idea. It was a very funny idea indeed, different from any other idea Old Man Rabbit had ever had before in all his life. It made him scratch his head with his left hind foot, and think and wonder, but it pleased him, too; it was such a very funny idea.

First he took off his muffler and then he put on his gingham apron. He took his best red table-cloth from the drawer and put it on his table and then he set the table with his gold banded china dinner set. By the time he had done all this, the pudding was boiled, so he lifted it, all sweet and steaming, from the kettle and set it in the middle of the table. Around the pudding, Old Man Rabbit piled heaps and heaps of corn and carrots and tur-nips and apples and potatoes, and then he took down his dinner bell that was all rusty because Old Man Rabbit had very seldom rung it before, and he stood in his front door and he rang it very hard, calling in a loud voice.

"Dinner's ready! Come to dinner, Billy Chipmunk, and Molly Mouse, and Tommy Chickadee!"

They all came, and they brought their friends with them. Tommy Chickadee brought Rusty Robin who had a broken wing and had not been able to fly South for the winter. Billy Chipmunk brought Chatter-Chee, a lame squirrel, whom he had invited to share his hole for a few months, and Molly Mouse brought a young gentleman Field Mouse, who was very distinguished looking because of his long whiskers. When they all tumbled into Old Man Rabbit's house and saw the table with the pudding in the center they forgot their manners and began eating as fast as they could, every one of them.

It kept Old Man Rabbit very busy waiting on them. He gave all the currants from the pudding to Tommy Chickadee and Rusty Robin. He selected juicy turnips for Molly Mouse and her friend, and the largest apples for Billy Chipmunk. Old Man Rabbit was so busy that he didn't have any time to eat a bite of dinner himself, but he didn't mind that, not one single bit. It made him feel so warm and full inside just to see the others eating.

When the dinner was over and not one single crumb was left on the table, Tommy Chickadee hopped up on the back of his chair and chirped.

"Three cheers for Old Man Rabbit's Thanksgiving dinner!"

"Hurrah, Hurrah," they all twittered and chirped and chattered. And Old Man Rabbit was so surprised that he didn't get over it for a week. You see he had really given a Thanksgiving dinner without knowing that it really and truly was Thanksgiving Day.

CAROLYN SHERWIN BAILEY.

THE GREAT STONE FACE

You had only to lift your eyes, and there it was plainly to be seen, though miles away, with the sunshine brightening all its features.

What was the Great Stone Face?

It seemed as if an enormous giant had sculptured his own likeness on a mountain side. There was the broad arch of the forehead, a hundred feet in height; the nose, with its long bridge; and the vast lips, which, if they could have spoken would have rolled in thunder from one end of the valley to the other. True it was that if you came too near, you lost the outline of the Face and could see only a heap of ponderous rocks, but when you retraced your steps, the wondrous features could be seen again, and the people who lived below it believed that their valley was so fertile because the Great Stone Face looked down upon it lighting up the clouds, and giving tenderness to the sunshine.

Now there was a little boy named Ernest who lived in the valley, and his mother had told him a story that her mother had told to her; a story so very old that even the Indians did not know who had first told it, unless it had been murmured by the mountain streams, and whispered by the wind among the tree tops. This was the story—that, sometime, a child should be born who would become the greatest and noblest person of his time, and his face, in manhood, should be the exact likeness of the Great Stone Face. But though the people had watched and waited until they were weary, no man greater and nobler than his neighbors had they yet beheld.

"Oh, mother, dear mother!" cried Ernest. "I do hope I shall live to see him."

"Perhaps you may," said his mother doubtfully.

And Ernest never forgot the story. It was

always in his mind whenever he looked upon the Great Stone Face. He grew up in the log cottage, and was dutiful to his mother, and helped her with his little hands and more with his loving heart. From a lad he became a quiet youth, sunbrowned from work in the fields, and well learned, though he never had any teacher except that Great Stone Face which smiled down upon him at night when his work was done.

About this time there went a rumor through the valley that the great man who was to bear a resemblance to the Great Stone Face, had appeared at last. His name was Gathergold, and he was a very rich merchant and owned a whole fleet of ships. All the countries of the world had added to his wealth. The cold regions of the North had sent him furs; hot Africa had gathered the ivory tusks of her great elephants out of the forests; the East had brought him spices and teas and diamonds and pearls. Mr. Gathergold had become so very rich that it would have taken him a hundred years to count his money so he decided to go back and end his days in the valley where he was born.

He ordered a wonderful palace of marble so dazzlingly white that it seemed as if it would melt in the sunshine. When the mansion was done, the upholsterers came with magnificent furniture, and then a whole troop of black and white servants who said that Mr. Gathergold would arrive at sunset.

"Here he comes," cried the people who were waiting to see him. "Here comes the great Mr. Gathergold!"

A carriage, drawn by four horses, dashed round the turn of the road. Within it sat a little old man with a skin as yellow as his own gold.

"The very image of the Great Stone Face!" shouted the people, but Ernest, who had been watching, too, turned sadly and looked up the valley, where, in the gathering mist, he could see the wonderful Face, and the lips seemed to say:

"He will come! Fear not, Ernest; the man will come."

The years went on, and Ernest was a young man, still good, and true, and kind. Poor Mr. Gathergold died and was buried, and the oddest part of the matter was that his wealth all disappeared before he died, leaving nothing of him but a skeleton covered with a wrinkled yellow skin; and every one decided that he had never borne the slightest resemblance to the Great Stone Face.

Then a warworn veteran, who had won great honors on the battlefield and was named Old Blood-and-Thunder decided to come back to the valley where he had been born. His neighbors resolved to welcome him with a salute of cannon and a public dinner, for they were all quite sure Old Blood-and-Thunder would bear the likeness of the Great Stone Face.

On the day of his arrival Ernest and all the others left their work and went out to meet Old-Blood-and-Thunder.

" 'Tis the same face, to a hair!" cried one man.

"Wonderfully like," cried another.

Then Ernest saw him. There he was, over the shoulders of the crowd with glittering epaulets and an embroidered collar and there, too, through the vista of the forest appeared the Great Stone Face.

"This is not he," thought Ernest.

More years passed. Ernest was now an older man. He still laboured for his bread, but he had done so much for his neighbors that it seemed as if he had been talking with the angels and had gotten a portion of their wisdom unawares.

The people of the Valley had found out—after a while—that Old Blood-and-Thunder's face had not the gentleness of the Great Stone Face and now they said, again, that its likeness was to appear upon the broad shoulders of a great statesman.

Old Stony Phiz, he was called, and while his friends were doing their best to make him President, he set out on a visit to the valley where he had been born.

Ernest and all the others went out to meet him. A cavalcade came prancing along the road, with a clattering of hoofs. There was a band of music, and while the people were throwing up their hats and shouting, an open barouche came by, drawn by four black horses. Inside with his massive head uncovered sat the great statesman, Old Stony Phiz, himself.

"Confess it," cried some one to Ernest. "The Great Stone Face has met its equal."

But Ernest turned away disappointed. The eyes and brow of the great man had none of the nobleness of the Face on the mountain side.

And Ernest grew to be an old man, but a strange thing happened. He was no longer an obscure husbandman. Men from the cities began coming to see him to learn from him the things that he had learned from the Great Stone Face, things not put down in books, and he was suddenly become famous.

One day a great Poet came to the Valley and stopped at Ernest's cottage to ask shelter for the night.

It was Ernest's custom each evening to talk to the assemblage of neighbors in a small nook among the hills near his cottage. To this spot he and the Poet went at sunset. All about was the pleasant foliage of many creeping plants, while Ernest's friends sat in the grove at his feet and in another direction could be seen the Great Stone Face with heavy mists about it, like the white leaves around the brow of Ernest.

At that moment Ernest's face, as he began to speak, grew wonderfully grand, and the Poet threw his arms aloft and shouted,

"Behold! Behold! Ernest is himself the likeness of the Great Stone Face."

Then all the people looked and saw that what the poet said was true. The prophecy was fulfilled.

Through the courtesy of Messrs. Houghton, Mifflin Company, authorized publishers of Nathaniel Hawthorne's works.

STORIES SELECTED BECAUSE EACH HAS A WELL-DEVELOPED CLIMAX

MR. FROG AND MR. ELEPHANT	*In Firelight Stories*
THE UGLY DUCKLING	*Hans Christian Andersen*
THE PRINCESS AND THE PEA	*Hans Christian Andersen*
THE HAPPY PRINCE	*Oscar Wilde*
LITTLE COSETTE	*Victor Hugo, in Les Misérables*
THE GOLDEN WINDOWS	

Laura E. Richards, in The Golden Windows

THE SHUT-UP-POSY *Annie Trumbull Slosson, in Story Tell Lib*

THE BOY THAT WAS SCARED OF DYING

Annie Trumbull Slosson, in Story Tell Lib

NAHUM PRINCE	*Edward Everett Hale*
THE ANXIOUS LEAF	*Henry Ward Beecher, in Norwood*
THE STONE IN THE ROAD	*In For the Children's Hour*

CHAPTER VI

TRAINING A CHILD'S MEMORY BY MEANS OF A STORY

IN the first place, what is the mental process by means of which we recall something stored in the cedar and lavender of our mind chests?

As you pass along a crowded city thoroughfare you are suddenly and unexpectedly confronted by an old friend. She steps out of a crowd of strangers and faces you. You recognize her at once as a bit of long-ago, changed with the years a bit but still, in a measure, familiar. You are unable though, for an instant's space, to recall your friend's name. In that instant's pause, however, a mental miracle takes place illuminating for us the process by means of which the human mind brings about a recall of an idea.

You clasp your friend's hand. You look

deep into her eyes. You note a similar perfume permeating her clothing that you knew in
former years. She speaks to you, and you
recognize the old, familiar quality of tone in
her voice. Then the miracle happens, and
your friend's name finds its way to your lips.
It is Mrs. B——. You had not really forgotten Mrs. B's name. It had been stored
away in a cobweb-hung corner of your mind
together with its mental associates; the *touch*
memories of her hand clasp, the *odor* memory
of her perfume, the *sound* memory of her
voice. As you again experience these touch,
odor and sound stimuli, Mrs. B's name rises in
their wake like a phœnix long buried in the
ashes of forgetfulness.

*Memory is a process of association of ideas.
Not repetition of an idea, but surrounding it
with a host of witnesses gives it permanency in
the mind.*

To a greater extent than can possibly be esti-
mated does this associative quality of memory
hold in the case of children. We wish to teach
a kindergarten child that a certain type of

flower is known as a *rose.* We do not repeat to him over and over again, or ask him to repeat to us, in order to fix this fact in his mind— *"This is a rose. This is a rose."* Instead, we ask him to smell of the flower, note its color, the shape of its petals, its peculiar, thorny stem, its leaves. We help the child to draw a picture of a rose. We ask him to show us all the roses he can find as we take him to walk in the garden. Then, when the child has the flower's color, odor, feeling, form and garden environment as a crowd of mind witnesses to prove its individuality, we say *"This is a rose,"* and the child is very apt to remember the flower.

A well-constructed child's story has the asso- ciative quality that characterizes the mental process of memorizing. It has one central theme; an act of heroism, a nature fact, a bit of natural history, a note of the fantastic or the humorous and around this central theme are grouped the story associates; the dialogue, the description, the sensory elements, the surprise of the climax, all of which fix indelibly in the mind this central theme around which the story is written.

Every well told story means an added possibility of a recall in the child's mind and strengthens the general process of memory.

Laura Richards' story of "The Pig Brother" illustrates the type of story for which the story teller should search in order to train a child's memory. The theme of the story, the idea that is to be made a fixture in the child's mind, is that of the value of *cleanliness,* and *order* in life. The treatment of the theme is constructive, a process of building up scenes and blocking out unessentials to strengthen and make permanent the theme in the child's mind.

"There was once a child who was untidy," the story begins.

With no wasting of time over details the child who hears the story is introduced to the theme. There follows a bit of description explaining the *kind* of untidiness of the little story hero, how he left his toys and boots scattered about his playroom, spilled ink and covered his pinafore with jam. Then the child is confronted by the Tidy Angel who tells him to go out in the garden and play with his brother while she puts his nursery back into its former state of orderliness. The child goes out to the garden but he is in a condition of wonder in regard to this brother whom he is to seek. He meets a squirrel in the garden path, and he asks it if it is his brother, but the squirrel denies all relationship to the child because of his untidiness. Then the child meets a wren, and asks it the same question, which the bird also indignantly denies because of the child's untidy appearance. The child then interrogates the Tommy Cat who scorns all thought of relationship to him, telling him to go and look at himself in a mirror. The climax of the story is found when the child meets a pig who promptly claims relationship with him and causes the child to go back to his playroom resolved to be tidy and orderly in the future.

The story has a memory value for children because it presents one idea with a number of related associates. The story theme of the unpleasant results of being untidy is never lost sight of, but is presented over and over again in a series of related scenes so differentiated, however, by their contrast as to make them permanent in the child's mind. We may take these different scenes in the order in which the author presents them, discovering that each forms a stone in the whole structure, differing in their value but all taking form and color from one theme.

Scene 1. The child hero is banished from his playroom and his toys as a result of his own acts.

Scene 2. The child finds that he has no part in the outside world of little wild creatures, also because of his untidy habits.

Scene 3. For the same self-inflicted reason, he is disowned by his friends, the birds.

Scene 4. His house friend, the cat, disowns him because his habits of personal cleanliness do not accord with her standards.

Scene 5. The child finds the natural consequence of his untidiness in his welcome by the despised pig which brings about his resolve to be clean and orderly, hereafter.

Each story scene, as shown in this analysis is carefully planned, having in mind a grouping of associated ideas that will strengthen and vivify the image made on the child's mind by the story theme. As a result the child who has heard the story of "The Pig Brother" has gained a store of associated ideas that will be recalled when some one asks him to pick up his toys or use care in eating. He will remember that squirrels and birds are orderly in their nest making, that his cat uses care in regard to her person, that there is a big, unseen force at work in the world that makes for order—whether one calls it an Angel, or not, it really exists—and he remembers that a disregard of this law of order means disaster to the law breaker. The child of the story escaped from the Pig. He may not be so fortunate if he breaks the law. So our real child turns over and examines and sorts and weighs his mental associates of the concept *untidiness,* and makes his own decision in the negative in a way that would not have been possible without the carefully associated scenes of the story.

This may seem an over fine analysis of one story but it will help us in judging other child stories having a regard to their memory value for the child.

Almost, if not more important a consideration than the writing of a drama, is the matter of the stage "business" in its successful production. The manager must decide which movements of his actors, which exits and entrances, which stage arrangement, lighting and what scheme of costuming will strengthen the salient idea underlying the plot of the drama and make it a *memory* in the minds of the audience. Stage "business" is a matter of psychology. It means that the stage manager, the playwright or whoever knows the audience best is going to plan a mechanical background, a hedge, a wall, of associates that will make the audience remember the play. A good story should have "business," the necessary costuming and lighting.

How shall the story teller apply this memory test in her selection of stories? How shall she be able to say with authority:

"My children will not forget this story!"

In the first place we should assure ourselves to our complete satisfaction in selecting a story that it *has a theme,* a *motif* upon which we can build the chords of a complete melody. It is doubtful if the story of "The Greedy Cat" has a sufficient theme to make it of value as a memory story, although it has a very real place in the child's life as a relaxing bit of nonsense. "The Little Pine Tree That Wished New Leaves" has a well defined theme—that of *contentment.*

The second question that we will ask ourselves will be, *is this story theme a worth while one for us to give the children as a permanent part of their mental lives?* We would hardly wish a child to remember always about the greed of the gormandizing cat. We would be glad to have him hang up in his mind house a picture of content as illustrated by the little green tree that discovered his own leaves to be better than any others.

Last, we will ask, *is the story theme so compellingly associated with other ideas that it will become a memory for the child?* In the case of the story of the Little Pine Tree, this treatment is carefully adhered to. Never is the *leaf* idea lost. Instead, the idea is presented in the form of gold leaves, leaves of glass, in fact all the strange and different leaves for which the discontented tree wished. But the gold leaves are stolen by a miser; the glass leaves are broken in a storm, and its juicy large leaves are all eaten by a goat. The climax is reached when the little tree is glad to have back its slender green needles; and the story is fixed in a child's mind because of its associative treatment.

This memory training by means of story telling is a legitimate "short cut" in teaching. The nature fact, that difficult bit of geography, that fine point of ethics may all be given a permanent place in the child's mind if we can find just the right story to help in fixing them. The list of stories that follows at the end of this chapter was selected having in mind in the case of each story, its associative treatment of one theme worth while as a memory for the child. Hans Andersen's story of Little Tuk is a brilliant example of using associated ideas to set the memory gem of the plot.

LITTLE TUK

Now there was little Tuk. As a matter of fact his name was not Tuk at all, but before he could speak properly he called himself Tuk. He meant it for Carl, so it is just as well we should know that. He had to look after his sister Gustave who was much smaller than he was, and then he had his lessons to do, but these two things were rather difficult to manage at the same time.

The poor little boy sat with his little sister in his lap, at the same time looking at his open geography book which he held in front of him. Before school time the next morning he had to know the names of all the towns by heart and everything there was to know about them.

At last his mother came home, for she had been out, and she took little Gustave. Tuk ran to the window and read as hard as he could, for it was growing dark fast, and his mother could not afford to buy candles.

"There's the old washerwoman from the lane," his mother said as she looked out of the window. "She can hardly carry herself, and yet she has to carry the pail from the pump. Run down, little Tuk, and be a dear boy. Help the old woman!"

Tuk jumped up at once and ran to help her, but when he got home again it was quite dark and it was useless to talk about candles. He had to go to bed. He had an old turn-up bed, and he lay in it, thinking about his geography lesson, the Island of Zealand, and all his teacher had told him about it. He ought to have been learning the lesson, but of course, he could not do that now. He put the geography book under his pillow and he lay there thinking, and thinking—and then all at once it seemed just as if some one had kissed him on his eyes and nose and mouth, and he fell asleep.

Yet he was not quite asleep either. It seemed to him as if the old washerwoman were looking at him with her kind eyes and saying,

"It would be a great shame if you were not to know your lesson. You helped me, and now I will help you."

And all at once the book under his head went "cribble, crabble."

"Cluck, cluck, cluck!" There stood a hen from the town of Kiöge.

"I am a Kiöge hen," it said, and then it went on to tell him how many inhabitants there were, and about the battle which had taken place there.

"Cribble, crabble, bang!" something plumped down; it was a wooden bird, the popinjay from Præstö. It told him that there were just as many inhabitants in Præstö as it had nails in its body, and it was very proud of this.

Now little Tuk no longer lay in bed. Gallop-a-gallop he went. He was sitting in front of a splendidly dressed knight with a shining helmet and a waving plume. They rode through the woods to the old town of Vordingborg, a very large and prosperous town. The castle towered above the royal city, and lights shone through the windows. There were songs and dancing within and the king was leading out the stately young court ladies to the dance. Morning came, and as the sun rose, the town sank away and the king's palace, one tower after the other. At last only a single tower remained on the hill where the castle had stood, and the town had become tiny and very poor. The schoolboys came along with their books under their arms, and they said, "two thousand inhabitants," but that was not true. There were not so many.

Little Tuk was still lying in his bed. First he thought he was dreaming, and then he thought he was not dreaming, but there was somebody close to him.

It was a sailor, a tiny little fellow, who might have been a cadet, and he said, "Little Tuk! Little Tuk! I greet you warmly from Korsöer which is a rising town. It is a flourishing town with steamers and coaches. It lies close to the sea and it has good high roads and pleasure gardens. It wanted to send a ship round the world but it did not do it, although it might have. And there is the most delicious scent about the town because there are beautiful rose gardens close by the gates."

Little Tuk saw them, the green and red flowering branches, and then they vanished before his eyes and changed into wooded heights sloping down to the clear waters of the fjord. A stately old church towered over the fjord with its twin spires. Springs of water rushed down in bubbling streams, close by them sat an old king with a golden crown round his flowing locks. It was King Kroar of the Springs, and little Tuk was in Rœskilde. Down over the slopes and past the springs walked hand in hand all Denmark's kings and queens wearing their crowns. On and on they went into the old church in time to the pealing of the bells and the rippling of the springs.

All at once everything vanished—where were they? Now an old peasant woman stood before little Tuk. She was a weeding woman and came from Sorö where the grass grows in the market place. She had put her gray linen apron over her head and shoulders. It was soaking wet; there must have been rain.

"Yes, indeed, it has been raining," she said. Then she suddenly shrank up and wagged her head. It looked as if she were about to take a leap.

"Koax," she said, "it is wet; it is wet; it is dull as ditch water—in good old Sorö." She had become a frog.

"Koax" and then once more she was the old woman.

"One must dress according to the weather," said she. "It is wet, it is wet. My town is like a bottle; you get in by the neck and you have to come out the same way again."

The old woman's voice sounded just like the croaking of frogs, or the creaking of fishing boots when you walk in the swamp. It was always the same sound, so tiresome, so tiresome that little Tuk fell into a deep sleep, which was the best thing for him.

But even in this sound sleep he had a dream, or something of the sort. His little sister, Gustave, with the blue eyes and golden, curly hair, had all at once become a lovely grown up girl and, without having wings, she could fly. So Gustave and Tuk flew together right across Zealand, over the green woods and deep blue waters.

"Do you hear the cock crowing, little Tuk? The hens come flying up from Kiöge town. You shall have such a big, big chicken yard. You will be a rich and happy man! Your house shall hold up its head like the king's towers, and be richly built up with marble statues like those in Præstö.

"Your name will spread round the world with praise like the ship which was to have sailed from Korsöer; and it will be known as far as Rœskilde town."

Little Tuk seemed to hear all this in his dreams, but he suddenly woke up. It was bright daylight, and he sprang out of bed and read his book. He found that he knew all the towns in his geography book almost at once.

The old washerwoman put her head in at the door, nodded to him and said—

"Many thanks for your help of yesterday, you

dear child. May you have the wish of your heart!"

But little Tuk hurried off to school with his book under his arm. He knew that he had already the wish of his heart—he had learned his geography lesson.

STORIES SELECTED BECAUSE OF THEIR STIMULUS TO A CHILD'S MEMORY

THE LITTLE PINE TREE THAT WISHED FOR NEW LEAVES
In For the Children's Hour
THE STORY OF THE MORNING GLORY SEED
Emilie Poulsson, in In the Child's World
THE SEED BABIES' BLANKET
Mary Gaylord, in For the Children's Hour
ABOUT ANGELS   *Laura Richards, in The Golden Windows*
THE CRY FAIRY   *Alice Brown, in The One-Footed Fairy*
THE DISAPPOINTED BUSH
Thornton Burgess, in Mother West Wind's Children
HOW THE CAMEL GOT HIS HUMP
Rudyard Kipling, in Just So Stories

CHAPTER VII

THE INSTINCT STORY

A NEWLY hatched chicken begins its daily work of living and providing for itself by scratching the earth in a phenomenally short space of time after it has chipped its shell. A baby notices a kitten and stretches out its hands to grasp in them a colored flower at almost the same period of its development as when it smiles at its mother. The chicken and the baby are alike in being creatures of *instinct*. The chicken scratches because its mother scratched for a living in the days of her chicken-hood and so did her mother and as many other hens and chickens as many previous years as one can count. The baby feels himself akin with the cat and loves the flower because his ancestors lived in close comradeship with animals and nature. From these and from an analysis of many other phases of instinct we may come at a working definition of the phenomenon.

Instinct may be defined as inherited memory.

It may be said that a child starts out on his life journey with a certain amount of brain capital which is his gift at birth. He has no knowledge of the outside world at birth. Color, sound, heat, cold and like concepts are unknown to him and he must make them his through the medium of his senses. The will to use his senses in the acquiring of useful information constitutes his brain capital, however. Instinctively he claims brotherhood with the animal world, and instinctively also he claims kinship with trees and flowers and winter and summer and birds and the gleaming earth. Pebbles and shells and sand and seeds interest him with a compellingness beyond our understanding until we remember that a child is the epitome of all the ages of the race which have combined to make us and our civilization. The age when man bartered with pebbles, decorated his person with shells, lived in a cave and found his food in seeds and berries is exemplified in the little chap at play on the beach with these same nature materials.

This mind capital of instinct with which the child comes into the world may be divided into the instinct to *express ideas in bodily movements, instinctive interest in animals and nature,* the *instinct* in *rhythm,* and the *instinct for self-preservation* (less highly developed in children than in animals.) There are other and finer divisions into which the different phases and manifestations of instinct fall but for purposes of our discussion these more elastic divisions will serve. The first division, the motor instinct, involves so much in the matter of a child's dramatizing of stories that it needs a chapter devoted wholly to a study of a child's bodily expression as stimulated by the images which he has in his mind. The instinct in rhythm, instinctive love of animals and nature, the self-preservation and curiosity instincts may be briefly considered in order of their appearance in the child's development, having in mind their influence upon the stories we select for a child's hearing. A financier makes it his special study to discover the best uses to which he can put his capital in order to make it produce for him appreciable dividends. The story teller, using the child mind capital, *instinct,* as a basis for her selection of stories will find that there are certain *instinct* stories that she may select for her use, each one of which gives back good returns to her along the measure of child interest.

Instinctive interest in rhythmic movements and rhythmic sounds is found in the very young child. He likes to be *trotted,* sung to in a monotonous, sing-song fashion; he enjoys clapping his hands in time to some nursery jingle or ditty. Long after this rhythmic period of babyhood is past children like to hear stories that have the rhythmic, repetitional quality, or some jingle introduced that stimulates rhythm. Predominantly is this rhythmic quality found in Mother Goose and folk lore. Children, even of kindergarten age, take the greatest delight in repeating and singing over and over again such rhythmic ditties as:

"Pitty, patty polt; shoe the wild colt.
Here a nail, there a nail, pitty, patty polt."

"Pat-a-cake, pat-a-cake, baker's man
Bake me a cake as fast as you can,
Pat it and prick it, and mark it with T,
And put it in the oven for Tommy and me."

"Intry, mintry, cutry corn,
Apple seed and apple thorn,
Wire, brier, limber, lock.
Three geese in a flock.
One flew East and one flew West,
And one flew over the black-bird's nest."

The appeal for the child in the case of all such jingles is a *bodily, instinctive* one. *This instinctive interest in rhythm is the beginning of bodily expression. The repetition of sounds, even though they are meaningless, makes the child feel the story.* It gets into his muscles, so to speak, if we may put a psychological fact into physiological terms.

Nearly all of the old folk tales are characterized by this rhythmic swinging-along mode of construction. We all know how children wait breathlessly, and then fairly bubble over with ecstatic mirth as they listen to "The Teeny Tiny Lady," "The House that Jack Built," and "The Kid Who Would Not Go." They literally wait spellbound for such phrases as:

"I'll huff, and I'll puff and I'll blow your house in."
The Three Little Pigs.

"First she leaped and then she ran,
Till she came to the cow and thus began."
The Cat and The Mouse.

"Fallen into the fire, and so will you,
On, little Drummikin, tum, tum, too."
The Story of Lambikin.

Sheer nonsense, we say? Possibly, for the ears of adults, but for a child it means instinct food. This doggerel verse belongs to a certain stage of his development just as folk songs and war songs of quite as strange content have come down to us from primitive races; and a very sure way of securing a child's involuntary attention to a story is to select it having in mind its rhythmic content.

Instinctive interest in animals and nature follows the rhythm instinct. This should not be construed into a statement that science and biology should be given children in the story form at an early age. Rather should the world about the child be presented to him on the plane of kinship, his one-ness with it. He is the little Hiawatha, friend of the trees, the deer, the birds, and the stars. Through this friendly introduction to the world of Nature, a child will come to know it, appreciate it, and eventually understand it.

The animal and nature stories that make the strongest appeal to the child's primitive nature instinct are those which, without mis-stating scientific facts, still make nature of a size with, friendly to, companionable with the child.

King of animal story tellers was Joel Chandler Harris. His "Nights With Uncle Remus" is a book of *instinct, race* stories. Bre'r Rabbit is an immortal *human* who walks side by side with a child, holding familiar intercourse with him and telling him the secrets of field and wood and stream. Rudyard Kipling, in the "Jungle Books" and the "Just So Stories" has met the *instinct* story needs of children by making the wild creatures of the jungle and desert vivid, human and companionable. The fables of the Chinese, of Bidpai and of Æsop have an instinctive interest for all children because they are human documents, an attempted explanation of the moral code, put quaintly by primitive races into the mouths of animals.

Nature stories that meet the *instinctive* interests of children are less easy for the story teller to find than are good animal stories. The modern nature story that is written about some dry scientific fact is only a bare husk when a child is crying for real food. It would be better to tell a child as a plain statement of a universal fact that the cold mercifully kills the plant that has served its use of reproduction of species that it may make way for another season's cycle of buds and blooms, than to tell a story about Jack Frost who, airily attired in white, skips about the garden and puts the flowers to sleep. Better, however, than this former bald statement of the year's au-

tumnal death that presages the awakening to
new life in the spring is it to tell children the
story of "Ceres and Persephone." Always,
afterward, will the bleak winter suggest to
their minds Persephone's sojourn with Pluto
and spring will herald her return to her
mother, the flowers springing up for gladness
wherever she steps.

*The myth meets every child's instinctive in-
terest.*

It is a type of story that has been left us
by every race and people as the explanation
that primitive minds made of natural phenomenon. Suppose a myth isn't true. Was
the Jack Frost story true; and isn't there more
real literature and imagery and inspiration in
the story of Persephone than in any modern
"Nature-faked" story? As a child stands on
Mount Olympus in company with the gods he
gets a vision of the universe that he would gain
in no other way. As he rides in Phaëton's
chariot searching for the Apples of Hesperides
and helps old Atlas hold the world upon his
shoulders he is learning Nature as no text-book

can teach her. As he listens to the murmur-
ing of the trees he hears the pipes of Pan and
the loving whispers of old Baucis and Philemon among their branches.

We will feed the child's instincts with the
old myths if we wish to secure his lasting interest in nature.

A trifle more difficult for the story teller to
meet is the child's instinct for self preserva-
tion. In the case of the lower animals this
instinct manifests itself in a perpetual warfare waged tooth and nail against its life ene-
mies, with a result epitomized, always, in the
survival of the stronger animal. Primitive
man waged a similar warfare. With a peace-
ful civilization this condition of individual
warfare has been done away with, but the instinct to fight for his rights, to preserve his *ego,*
to keep selfishly for his own certain *things* is
a part of the child's mental heritage from his
forbears. The rhythm instinct, the *Nature* instinct are the gold mine in child development.
The *self* instinct, while in a measure necessary
in fitting a child for the life struggle, should

131

be, to a certain extent, inhibited. This inhibition may be brought about through the medium of stories.

Selecting just the right ethical stories to tell a child having in mind making him unselfish is a delicate matter. Each story should present some problem in ethics that is likely to come up in the child's life. Moreover, the moral of the story should be veiled but made so obvious by the suspensive treatment and climax of the story, that the child unconsciously makes it his own and applies the lesson to his own life. The moral of unselfishness is rather the *result* of the story than a part of it as the children make its obvious application to their own lives.

The well-known folk tale of "The Little Red Hen" teaches a lesson of unselfishness. The selfish pig, cat and frog are deprived of their portion of the freshly baked loaf of bread because they had no share in its making. Kipling's story, "How the Camel Got his Hump" in the "Just So Stories" has the same moral of forgetfulness of self. Laura E. Richards' story, "The Coming of the

King," beautifully illustrates the type of story that inhibits the selfish instinct. It draws a wonderful word picture of the children's garden made ready for the King and finally welcoming a beggar in ministering to whose needs, however, the children find joy.

The most classic of *unselfish* stories in the English language is Oscar Wilde's "Selfish Giant." It needs no word of introduction or explanation. It illuminates our dull subject of endeavoring to make children self forgetful through the stimulus of the ethical story.

THE SELFISH GIANT

Every afternoon, as they were coming from school, the children used to go and play in the Giant's garden.

It was a large, lovely garden, with soft green grass. Here and there over the grass stood beautiful flowers like stars, and there were twelve peach trees that in the springtime broke out into delicate blossoms of pink and pearl, and in the autumn bore rich fruit. The birds sat on the trees and sang so sweetly that the children used to stop their games in order to listen to them. "How happy we are here!" they cried to each other.

One day the Giant came back. He had been to visit his friend, the Cornish ogre, and had stayed with him for seven years. After the seven years were over he had said all that he had to say, for his conversation was limited, and he determined to return to his own castle. When he arrived he saw the children playing in the garden.

"What are you doing there?" he cried in a very gruff voice, and the children ran away.

"My own garden is my own garden," said the Giant; "any one can understand that, and I will allow nobody to play in it but myself." So he built a high wall all round it, and put up a notice-board.

> TRESPASSERS
> WILL BE
> PROSECUTED.

He was a very selfish giant.

The poor children had now nowhere to play. They tried to play on the road, but the road was very dusty and full of hard stones, and they did not like it. They used to wander round the high wall when their lessons were over, and talk about the beautiful garden inside. "How happy we were there," they said to each other.

Then the spring came, and all over the country there were little blossoms and little birds. Only in the garden of the Selfish Giant it was still winter. The birds did not care to sing in it as there were no children, and the trees forgot to blossom. Once a beautiful flower put its head out from the grass, but when it saw the notice-board it was so sorry for the children that it slipped back into the ground again, and went off to sleep. The only people who were pleased were the Snow and the Frost. "Spring has forgotten this garden," they cried, "so we will live here all the year round." The Snow covered up the grass with her great white cloak, and the Frost painted all the trees silver. Then they invited the North Wind to stay with them, and he came. He was wrapped in furs, and he roared all day about the garden, and blew the the chimney-pots down. "This is a delightful spot," he said, "we must ask the Hail on a visit." So the Hail came. Every day for three hours he rattled on the roof of the castle till he broke most of the slates, and then he ran round and round the garden as fast as he could go. He was dressed in gray, and his breath was like ice.

"I cannot understand why the spring is so late in coming," said the Selfish Giant, as he sat at the

window and looked out at his cold white garden;
"I hope there will be a change in the weather."

But the spring never came, nor the summer.
The autumn gave golden fruit to every garden,
but to the Giant's garden none. "He is too selfish," she said. So it was always winter there, and
the North Wind, and the Hail, and the Frost, and
the Snow danced about through the trees.

One morning the Giant was lying awake in bed
when he heard some lovely music. It sounded so
sweet to his ears that he thought it must be the
King's musicians passing by. It was really only a
little linnet singing outside his window but it was
so long since he had heard a bird sing in his garden
that it seemed to him to be the most beautiful music in the world. Then the Hail stopped
dancing over his head, and the North Wind ceased
roaring, and a delicious perfume came to him
through the open casement. "I believe the spring
has come at last," said the Giant; and he jumped
out of bed and looked out.

What did he see?

He saw a most wonderful sight. Through a
little hole in the wall the children had crept in, and
they were sitting in the branches of the trees. In
every tree that he could see there was a little child.
And the trees were so glad to have the children

back again that they had covered themselves with blossoms, and were waving their arms gently above the children's heads. The birds were flying about and twittering with delight, and the flowers were looking up through the green grass and laughing. It was a lovely scene, only in one corner it was still winter. It was the farthest corner of the garden, and in it was standing a little boy. He was so small that he could not reach up to the branches of the tree, and he was wandering all round it, crying bitterly. The poor tree was still quite covered with frost and snow, and the North Wind was blowing and roaring above it. "Climb up! little boy," said the Tree, and it bent its branches down as low as it could; but the boy was too tiny.

And the Giant's heart melted as he looked out. "How selfish I have been!" he said; "now I know why the spring would not come here. I will put that poor little boy on the top of the tree, and then I will knock down the wall, and my garden shall be the children's playground for ever and ever." He was really very sorry for what he had done.

So he crept downstairs and opened the front door quite softly, and went out into the garden. But when the children saw him they were so frightened that they all ran away, and the garden became winter again. Only the little boy did not run, for his eyes were so full of tears that he did not see the Giant coming. And the Giant strode up behind him and took him gently in his hand, and put him up into the tree. And the tree broke at once into blossom, and the birds came and sang on it, and the little boy stretched out his two arms and flung them around the Giant's neck, and kissed him. And the other children, when they saw that the Giant was not wicked any longer, came running back, and with them came the spring. "It is your garden now, little children," said the Giant, and he took a great axe and knocked down the wall. And when the people were going to market at twelve o'clock they found the Giant playing with the children in the most beautiful garden they had ever seen.

All day long they played, and in the evening they came to the Giant to bid him good-by.

"But where is your little companion?" he said: "the boy I put into the tree." The Giant loved him the best because he had kissed him.

"We don't know," answered the children; "he has gone away."

"You must tell him to be sure and come here to-morrow," said the Giant. But the children said that they did not know where he lived, and had never seen him before; and the Giant felt very sad.

Every afternoon, when school was over, the children came and played with the Giant. But the little boy whom the Giant loved was never seen again. The giant was very kind to all the children, yet he longed for his first little friend, and often spoke of him. "How I would like to see him!" he used to say.

Years went over, and the Giant grew very old and feeble. He could not play about any more, so he sat in a huge armchair, and watched the children at their games, and admired his garden. "I have many beautiful flowers," he said, "but the children are the most beautiful flowers of all."

One winter morning he looked out of his window as he was dressing. He did not hate the winter now, for he knew that it was merely the spring asleep, and that the flowers were resting.

Suddenly he rubbed his eyes in wonder, and looked and looked. It certainly was a marvellous sight. In the farthest corner of the garden was a tree quite covered with lovely white blossoms. Its branches were all golden, and silver fruit hung down from them, and underneath it stood the little boy he had loved.

Downstairs ran the Giant in great joy, and out

into the garden. He hastened across the grass, and came near to the child. And when he came quite close his face grew red with anger, and he said, "Who hath dared to wound thee?" For on the palms of the child's hands were the prints of two nails, and the prints of two nails were on the little feet.

"Who hath dared to wound thee?" cried the Giant; "tell me, that I may take my big sword and slay him."

"Nay!" answered the child; "but these are the wounds of Love."

"Who art thou?" said the Giant, and a strange awe fell on him, and he knelt before the little child.

And the child smiled on the Giant, and said to him, "You let me play once in your garden, to-day you shall come with me to my garden, which is Paradise."

And when the children ran in that afternoon, they found the Giant lying dead under the tree, all covered with white blossoms.

OSCAR WILDE.

THE INSTINCT STORY

STORIES SELECTED BECAUSE OF THEIR INSTINCTIVE
INTEREST

RHYTHMIC STORIES:

THE HOUSE THAT JACK BUILT	*Mother Goose*
THE KID THAT WOULD NOT GO	*Folk Tale*
THE STORY OF LAMBIKIN	*In Firelight Stories*
THE TEENY TINY LADY	*In Firelight Stories*
THE STORY OF EPAMINONDAS AND HIS AUNTIE	

Sara Cone Bryant, in Best Stories to Tell to Children

ANIMAL STORIES AND MYTHS:

NIGHTS WITH UNCLE REMUS	*Joel Chandler Harris*
THE JUNGLE BOOKS	*Rudyard Kipling*
THE JUST-SO-STORIES	*Rudyard Kipling*
THE TALKING BEASTS	

Kate Douglas Wiggin and Nora Archibald Smith

THE LITTLE RED HEN	*In For the Children's Hour*
MYTHS EVERY CHILD SHOULD KNOW	*Hamilton Mabie*

STORIES TO INHIBIT THE SELFISH INSTINCT:

THE LITTLE RED HEN	*In For the Children's Hour*
THE COMING OF THE KING	

Laura E. Richards, in The Golden Windows

THE COOKY	*Laura E. Richards, in The Golden Windows*
THE STORY OF BABOUSCKA	*In For the Children's Hour*
THE LEGEND OF THE WOODPECKER	

In For the Children's Hour

PICCIOLA   *Celia Thaxter, in Stories and Poems for Children*

CHAPTER VIII

THE DRAMATIC STORY

IN the previous chapter we analyzed certain primitive phases of mental life as manifested in the instinctive acts of children. These manifestations of instinct form a basis for our story selection, guiding us toward a final and certain goal of child interest.

One phase of instinct was left out of our discussion except as it was touched upon primarily in the analysis of a child's instinctive interest in rhythm. This is the instinct to express through bodily movements the ideas that have found a permanent place for themselves in the mind.

Little E, three years old, was told by her nurse the folk tale of "The Old Woman and Her Pig." She had heard very few stories, and this one seemed to delight her beyond words. She laughed and clapped her hands over it, and begged to have it repeated and re-told even a third time. She made no comment upon the text of the story, however. A week later, she was left alone in her nursery for a short period during the morning and her mother, busy with household duties upon the floor below, thought that she heard E's voice. Going, quietly, to the door of the nursery she saw E standing, dramatically, in the center of the room, holding a toy broom under her arm, and shaking her finger at a small china pig that stood on the floor in front of her. As she did this, she said in the exact words of the story that had been told her:

"Piggy won't get over the stile, and I shall not get home to-night."

"What are you doing, E?" her mother asked in some surprise.

E looked up in wonder as if she, herself, knew a reason for her actions but one that needed no explanation. Finally she spoke:

"I'm *doing* a story, mother," she replied.

This incident of E's instinctive and almost unconscious dramatization of a story which she had heard and whose images had become fixed in her mind illustrates a very common characteristic of a child's mental life, the instinctive impulse to vitalize the mental life by putting it into terms of *expression*. It is true that instinctive expression as commonly defined includes in its first manifestations only certain *unlearned* motor responses, those forms of expression that are ours without previous training or experience. A child cries at a pain, laughs when he is tickled, starts in fear at a sudden and loud noise. These are the primitive forms of instinctive expression, but beyond these and through the use of certain child stories that are full of action, compelling dialogue, and quick movement comes a development of the dramatic instinct in childhood of wonderful value to the teacher.

Why do we want to make use of the dramatic instinct in childhood?

First, because this instinct to *do,* to *act,* to *express* is so common a part of each child's mental content upon entering school that it forms part of our previously discussed child brain capital. The instinct to *do* a story, to

144

give it expression in terms of bodily movement would not be given a child unless it had some value for the educator.

Second, we want to utilize the dramatic instinct of childhood, because it is a very sure way of helping a child to gain *poise, self-control,* and a complete *mastery of his environment.* The ability to give adequate expression through speech or action to the mental life characterizes the well-developed individual as opposed to the victim of self-consciousness. It means grace of body and freedom of verbal expression.

What qualities differentiate the dramatic child story from that story which is not as well adaptable for child acting?

Primarily, the story that we select for purposes of dramatization should have the quality of being *visual*—that is, it should be so full of simple, pictorial scenes, episodes and events that it will bring to the minds of the children a definite sequence of word pictures, stimulative to action. This "moving picture" quality is found in the old folk tales, the fables of Æsop and La Fontaine. Here the stage setting of the stories is simple and easily pictured by the child listeners. The story events find an immediate and permanent place in the child's mind and a possible outlet in action because of their apperceptive quality.

The story of "The Little Red Hen" is an interesting type of the story that lends itself to child dramatizing because of its *visual* quality. There is a series of home scenes; the little Red Hen's garden, her house, her kitchen, all familiar and easily seen by children but illuminated with the interest of mystery because of the Hen, herself, and her friends, the Cat and the Frog. "The Elves and the Shoemaker" is also a good story for child acting, while among the most dramatic visual fables are "The Town Mouse and The Country Mouse," "The Lion and the Mouse," "The Lark and Her Young Ones" and "The Hare and the Tortoise."

The second quality that the story teller should have in mind in selecting stories for child dramatizing is *simplicity* of dialogue. The story actors should converse, if not in childlike manner, at least in a simple, easy-to-understand vocabulary that will add to a child's store of words but will not tax him too much in reproduction. Here, again, we must turn to folk tales and fables for simple, straightforward, rich dialogue. Quite naturally and without apparent effort children verbalize the dialogue of "The Little Red Hen" after hearing the story once or twice.

"Who will build my fire?" she said.
"Not I!" said the Frog.
"Not I!" said the Cat.
"Then I will," said the Little Red Hen.

These and the other bits of simple dialogue that go to make up the plot of this story; the conversation between the Wolf and the Pig in the story of "The Three Little Pigs," the Lark and her little ones, Jack and the different characters in the Beanstalk story, the "Lion and the Mouse"—these are all examples of easily reproduced dialogue, stimulating spontaneous dialogue on the part of the children.

One further consideration in connection with the dramatic story—*spontaneity*.

Because of the popularity of so-called story dramatization among kindergartners and primary teachers, a school of child acting in kindergartens and the grades has sprung into life. Stories are dramatized *for* children rather than *by* the children themselves, and the results obtained through unnecessary costuming, certain stage properties and memorized dialogue are of no appreciable value in the mental development of the child. A child impersonates a pig gifted with human attributes, spontaneously, but he plays the part of a dressed-up fairy in a wooden, unspontaneous fashion. The difference between the two is just the difference between instinctive expression and prescribed action. In his "Principles of Psychology," Professor Thorndyke says:

"Given any mental state, that movement will be made which the inborn constitution of the nervous system has connected with the mental state or part of it. The baby reaches for a bright object because, by inner organization, that sense presentation is connected with that act. For the same reason he puts an object into his mouth when he feels it within his grasp. The boy puts up his arm and wards off a blow because his brain is so organized as to connect those responses with those situations.

"Given any mental state, that movement will be made which has been connected with it or part of it most frequently, most recently, in the most vivid experience and with the most satisfying results."

This careful and concrete statement of the law governing instinctive movement gives us our cue for selecting stories for child dramatizing and our method in presenting them, having in view—not child *acting*, but spontaneous child *action*. We will provide no costumes for our children, set no stage, but only give them that story which will suggest to them a recent, frequently repeated, vivid experience with its accompanying satisfying results in certain spontaneous movements.

Suppose we illustrate with a possible, voluntary dramatizing of the old and well loved folk tale of "The Gingerbread Boy." The experiences suggested to children by this story and suggesting action to them are *the chase* and the sense stimulus of *food*. After hearing the story a number of times until they are quite familiar with its dialogue and its characters and its sequence of episodes, the teacher may suggest to the children that they *play* it. A disastrous way to begin the play would be to assign the different characters in the story to different children, showing them where to stand or asking them to try and use the exact words that the story characters did. Rather should the dramatizing of the story be a developing process on the part of the teacher. If she has made the story permanent in the minds of the children, their rendering of it in action will be free and their dialogue spontaneous.

"Who wants to be the Gingerbread Boy?

"Who would like to be the Gingerbread Boy's mother?

"I see a child with very bright, sharp eyes. Is he not the Fox?

"We will need many Mowers and some Threshers.

"Who is the Pig, and who the Cow?"

These or similar hints on the part of the teacher are cues for the opening of the play— all that is needed, usually, to start the spontaneous dramatization. As naturally as if she were the story character herself, the little old woman mother rolls and pats the Gingerbread Boy into shape, puts him in an imaginary oven and then falls asleep. He makes his escape, is interviewed in turn by the Threshers, the Mowers, the Pig and the Cow, makes his escape from them also, only to be eventually captured and eaten by the Fox. As the story play goes on, it will be discovered that the child actors are rendering with perfect diction the dialogue of the story, enriching their vocabulary and gaining power of verbal expression. It will be discovered also that their movements are illustrative of the story, and absolutely lacking in self consciousness, typical of an added quota of poise and self-control gained through the play. Certain *responses* are always made to certain mind *situations*. What need is there of stage setting since a child actor sees in his mind's eye the barn full of Mowers whose mouths are watering to eat him up? Why should the tired-out teacher spend long after-school hours sewing together costumes when, at an instant's notice, a child is able to clothe himself in the sleek red coat and valiant brush of a fox?

It is to be questioned if the books of so-called dramatic stories for children which may be obtained now are really educational or have for their place upon the teacher's desk a firm psychologic background. Most of them seem to have for their scheme of compiling child *acting,* not *action.* The child on the stage is not developing mentally. Rather is he a mentally starved puppet, moved about by the wires of the stage and repeating lines in parrot-like fashion. The little girl, E, quoted at the beginning is an example of mental growth through spontaneous action. So the books of dramatic stories seem to have been prepared having in mind what the child should *say* or *do,* rather than presenting such interesting story material in such interesting form that a child will *speak* and *do* without any further stimulus than that of the story itself.

In selecting our stories for child dramatizing we will go to original sources and choose only such stories as are so rich in homely, apperceptive incidents, and so marked by possibilities for simple, interpretive dialogue as to lend themselves to instinctive action on the part of the children.

THE GINGERBREAD BOY

AS DRAMATIZED BY A GROUP OF CHILDREN

The Actors:
    A Little Old Woman.
    A Little Old Man.
    Some Mowers.
    Some Threshers.
    A Pig.
    A Fox.
    The Gingerbread Boy.

ACT I

Place: A Kitchen.
Time: Saturday Morning.
The Little Old Man Sits in a corner.

The Little Old Woman is seen, too, stirring cake dough and singing as she stirs:

> "Sugar, and spice, and everything nice—
> That's what a little girl's made of;
> Snaps, and snails, and puppy dogs' tails;
> That's what a little boy's made of!

"Ah, well-a-day, but I wish I had a little boy for all that! Some one to run to the store, and bring in the kindlings, and drive the cows to pasture, and feed the pig, and get into mischief, and be rocked to sleep in the evening."

She calls to the Little Old Man:

"Father! Oh, I say, Father! Fetch me the jug of molasses from the pantry. I am making a gingerbread cake for your supper!"

The Little Old Man does not move, or stir.

The Little Old Woman calls louder: "Fetch me the molasses jug, Father!"

The Little Old Woman crosses to the chimney corner, and shakes the Little Old Man, but he is asleep and does not wake.

The Little Old Woman holds up her hands in despair.

"Dearie me! I might as well have a broom for a Goodman as he. There is nothing done in the house unless I attend to it myself," she says.

She leaves the kitchen for a moment, returning

with the jug of molasses. She pours some molasses into the bowl, stirs again, and finally empties the dough out upon the board, rolling it flat with her rolling pin. Suddenly she stops, rolling pin in air.

The Little Old Woman: "I have it! I will make me a Gingerbread Boy!"

She works very fast, talking as she shapes the Gingerbread Boy with her fingers.

The Little Old Woman: "Here is his dear little head, with currants for eyes, and one raisin for his nose, and three raisins for his mouth. Here is his fine little jacket with a row of currants for buttons; and here are his two fine, fat little legs. Here are his arms, and here are his shoes!"

She lays the completed Gingerbread Boy in the baking pan and dances about the kitchen with it in her hands, singing as she dances, the Song of the Gingerbread Man:

"Hickory, dickory, dickory, dan;
Heigho, I sing for a Gingerbread Man!
Currants for eyes, and a round raisin nose,
Gingerbread shoes on his gingerbread toes,
Gingerbread jacket, so tight and neat,
Gingerbread smiles on his face so sweet,
Hickory, dickory, dickory, dan;
Heigho, I sing for a Gingerbread Man!"

As she finishes her song, she opens the imaginary oven door, and, kneeling down, puts in the tin which holds the Gingerbread Boy. Then she shakes the Little Old Man again.

The Little Old Woman: "Wake up, I say, Father! *Wake up! Wake up!* The garden's to be weeded, and the butter's to be churned! Wake up, I say, and mind the oven. There's a fine little Gingerbread Boy baking inside!"

The Little Old Man wakes very slowly, and looking all about the kitchen says in a dazed sort of way: "What's that you say, Mother? I don't see any little Gingerbread Boy."

The Little Old Woman goes to the stove and points to the oven. "He's in here baking. Do you mind him while I'm away. In twenty minutes by the clock, do you open the oven door, and the Gingerbread Boy will be baked."

The Little Old Man: "Yes, yes, Mother. Do you go and weed the garden and churn. I'll sit here, and mind the oven."

The Little Old Woman leaves the kitchen. After she has gone, the Little Old Man re-lights his pipe. Then he gets up from his chair and peeps in the oven door.

The Little Old Man: "A fine, fat Boy! A very fine, fat Gingerbread Boy! How his buttons shine, and he is swelling so much that his jacket is splitting. I shall eat him for my supper!"

He goes back to his chair, and begins smoking, but soon his head nods. He looks up at the clock.

The Little Old Man: "In twenty minutes I will take him out. I think I shall have a short nap in the meantime."

The Little Old Man falls fast asleep again, his pipe falling to the floor. As he sleeps, the oven door opens a little as if some one had pushed it from the inside. The real Gingerbread Boy peeps out through the crack. When he sees that the Little Old Man is asleep, he steps out. He begins blowing on his fingers and he puts them in his mouth as if they were burned. He fans himself with the baking tin which he brings with him out of the oven, and he hops about the kitchen on the tips of his toes.

The Gingerbread Boy: "My, but that oven was warm! I might have been burned to a crisp before any one remembered to take me out. So this is my new home!"

He looks about in all the corners of the kitchen.

"And *this* is my new father!"

He goes over to the Little Old Man, and pulls his wig. Then he sits down, cross-legged on the hearth, and goes on talking to himself.

The Gingerbread Boy: "I don't know whether I want to live in this house or not. I know what little boys have to do."

He counts on his fingers:

"They have to run to the store, and bring in kindlings, and drive the cows and feed the pigs. I'd rather have a good time. I think I will run away."

He jumps up, and looks around the room, cautiously.

"There's nobody here to see me go. Hurrah! Hurrah! Here I go, off by myself to see the world!"

He runs lightly out of the kitchen.

Act II

Place: A country road. The Gingerbread Boy is discovered, sitting on top of the wall, talking to himself.

The Gingerbread Boy: "Here I am, out by myself, seeing the world. The world's a very pleasant place, only I do wish I were not made of gingerbread, and I do wish that everybody wasn't so hungry. Wherever I travel some one wants to eat me. Bless my buttons, there comes some one now!"

The Mowers come slowly along with their

scythes over their shoulders. They sing as they walk:

> "On Chopnose Day the Mowers rise,
> As every one supposes,
> And march upon the grass and flowers,
> And cut off all their noses."

Suddenly the Mowers discover the Gingerbread Boy.

First Mower: "Who sits there on top of the wall?"

Second Mower: "It is a little boy made of gingerbread."

First Mower: "Let us eat him!"

Second Mower, going up to the Gingerbread Boy: "Good morning, my lad, where do you come from, and where are you going this fine morning?"

The Gingerbread Boy hops down from the wall, and dances away on the tips of his toes:

> "I've run away from a Little Old Woman,
> And a Little Old Man.
> I can run away from you, I can!
> Run, run, as fast as you can,
> You can't catch me,
> I'm the Gingerbread Man!"

He disappears, followed by the Mowers, but reappears at the other end of the road, looking frightened and out of breath.

The Gingerbread Boy: "They didn't catch me that time, but you never can tell what's going to happen next. There comes somebody else."

The Threshers are seen passing with their flails over their backs.

One of the Threshers: "Who is that by the side of the road?"

A Second Thresher: "That is a Gingerbread Boy!"

Both of the Threshers, going up to the Gingerbread Boy very fiercely: "Come with us and be eaten, my lad!"

The Gingerbread Boy dances a little way ahead of the Threshers as he calls back to them:

> "I've run away from a Little Old Woman,
> And a Little Old Man,
> Some Mowers—and—
> I can run away from you, I can.
> Run, run, as fast as you can,
> You can't catch me,
> I'm the Gingerbread Man."

He runs away a second time, followed by the Threshers, but he is seen in a moment at the end of the road. He climbs up on the wall again.

The Gingerbread Boy: "I wonder who will try and eat me next!"

He puts his hand up to his eyes. "There comes some one now!"

The Pig enters, grunting.

The Pig:

"One of us went to market; and one of us stayed at home.
One of us had roast beef, but I'm the Pig who had *none!*"

"I'm hungry enough to eat green apples. Ahe! What do I see? A Gingerbread Boy!" He walks up to the wall, and stands on his back feet, but he cannot reach to the top. The Gingerbread Boy dances on top of the wall.

"I've run away from a Little Old Woman,
And a Little Old Man,
Some Mowers, some Threshers—and—
I can get away from you, I can.
Jump, jump, as high as you can,
You can't catch me,
I'm the Gingerbread Man!"

The Pig tries to get the Gingerbread Boy, but he is not able to, and he walks away, still grunting.

The Gingerbread Boy: "Well, he didn't get me. I believe I am able to take care of myself after all. Why, who is that great creature, coming down the road?"

The Fox enters. He sees the Gingerbread Boy, but he pretends that he does not. He sits down and waits. The Gingerbread Boy watches the Fox. Then he speaks to him.

> "I've run away from a Little Old Woman,
> A Little Old Man,
> *Some Mowers, some Threshers, a Pig—and—*
> I can run away from you, I can!"

the Gingerbread Boy says.

The Fox speaks in a deep, gruff voice, without moving.

The Fox: "Step a little closer, Sonny. I'm very hard of hearing."

The Gingerbread Boy jumps down from the wall, and goes quite close to the Fox, speaking very loudly:

> *"I've run away from a Little Old Woman,*
> *A Little Old Man.*
> *Some Mowers, some Threshers, a Pig—and—*
> *I can run away from you, I can!"*

The Fox speaks again, without moving.

The Fox: "You will have to step closer yet, Sonny, I'm very, very hard of hearing."

The Gingerbread Boy goes up to the Fox, shouting in his ear. As he does so, the Fox eats him up.

The Town Mouse and the Country Mouse

Characters in the Play:

A Mouse Who Lives in Town.

A Mouse Who Lives in the Country.

Some other Mice, as many as one wishes, who live in the same hole as the country mouse. They include his Father, his Mother, and a number of Brothers and Sisters; a Cat.

THE FIRST PART OF THE STORY

Place: A mouse hole in a barn.

Time: The early evening of a day in the fall.

The Father, Mother, and younger mice are seen, sitting about, and nibbling bits of candles, turnips, carrots, and other dainties.

The Father, taking a large bite of turnip, and speaking between mouthfuls:

"I have been a mile to the south and a mile back to-day without meeting an enemy. I found a field of corn, and a garden of turnips, and a patch of large, juicy cabbages. For a comfortable, fat old age, there is no place like the country."

The Mother, running about very nimbly, and gathering up all the candle ends:

"You are right, Father. The farmer's wife

cleaned the candlesticks to-day, and she threw away all these ends. This evening I shall make a large tallow pudding!"

One of the younger Mice, who jumps up, and begins dancing very gracefully about the mouse hole on the tips of her toes:

"Everybody goes to bed so very, very early in the country. A mouse may dance until morning without being caught."

As she dances, the other Mice drop whatever they were eating, and they sing in funny, squeaking voices, a tune to which her feet keep time. This is their song:

> "Squeak, squeak, skip, skip!
> Gather your tail up, and trip, trip!
> Crickets and grasshoppers dance by day,
> But night is the time for a mouse to play,
> When the moon shines round, like a great big cheese—
> When only the sleepy Sand Man sees—
> Then—Squeak, squeak, skip, skip!
> Gather your tails up, and trip, trip!"

When the Mice finish their song, the Father looks all about the hole. Then he speaks.

The Father: "I do not see your brother. Where is your brother?"

The Mother, peering about in all the dark corners of the mouse hole: "Where is my son? Oh, where is my son?"

All the younger Mice, speaking together: "Oh, where is our brother?"

As the younger Mice speak, the Country Mouse enters at the back of the mouse hole. He wears a large red necktie which has green spots, and is tied in a bow in front. He seems to be very much excited. All the Mice crowd about him.

The Father, taking the Country Mouse by his paw and leading him to the front of the mouse hole:

"Where have you been all day, my son?"

The Mother, re-tying the Country Mouse's necktie: "You seem out of breath, my dear!"

All the younger Mice, excitedly: "Where have you been? Oh, do tell us where you have been?"

The Country Mouse: "I have had an adventure. I started out early this morning for the dairy, because I heard some one say that there were cheeses being made. On the way to the dairy I met a very fine Mouse, passing by on his way to town. He lives in the town, and he told me all about his home."

All the younger Mice, crowding closer that they may hear what the Country Mouse is saying:

"What did the Town Mouse tell you about his home?"

The Country Mouse: "He said that he lived in a pantry!"

The Father: "A pantry?"

The Mother: "A pantry?"

All the younger Mice: "A pantry?"

The Country Mouse: "Yes, a pantry! There are pies there, and cakes. There are fat hams, and juicy spare ribs. There are puddings, and there are cheese rinds lying about on the shelves. The servants are careless, and at night they leave the food uncovered. Then the Town Mouse comes out of the wall and sits on the pantry table, and eats his fill.

"No cold gardens to be searched for food. No frozen fields to be dug over for roots and corn stalks."

The Country Mouse looks disdainfully about the hole. Then he goes on speaking.

The Country Mouse: "The Town Mouse invited me to come and visit him this evening!"

The Younger Mice: "Oh!"

The Father, shaking his head, doubtfully: "Don't go, my boy. There is a wild animal who lives in town houses. She has eyes as large as saucers. She wears cushions on her feet that no one may hear her when she walks. She has sharp claws d sharper teeth. She can see in the dark."

166

The Mother: "It is the Cat! Don't go to town, my son. The Cat eats mice!"

The Country Mouse: "I am not afraid of the Cat. I am tired of this dull life in the country. I want to see sights, and taste the good things that are to be found in pantries. I am going, to-night, to visit the Town Mouse!"

The Father, Mother, and all the younger Mice try to hold the Country Mouse, but he gets away from them. He runs away through the back of the mouse hole.

THE SECOND PART OF THE STORY

Place: A pantry.

The Town Mouse sits on the edge of the table, eating, but nervously, and looking all about him as he nibbles.

Under one of the shelves, and behind the Town Mouse, so that he is not able to see her, sits the Cat.

Time: Midnight of the same evening.

The Cat plays that she is asleep, but she is really watching the Town Mouse. Suddenly she sneezes.

The Town Mouse, dropping a large piece of cheese, which he has been eating, and looking around in a frightened way:

"Oh, my ears and whiskers! Is that a sneeze which I hear?"

He trembles and shakes violently. He sees no one, though, so he picks up the cheese in one paw and a slice of bread in the other. As he nibbles, he talks to himself.

The Town Mouse: "I am tired of this life in town. Late suppers, and rich food to disturb one's digestion; traps, traps everywhere—wooden traps, and wire traps, round traps, and square traps; traps with doors, and traps with windows—and always a Cat hiding in a corner. She may be in the room now for all I know.

"To-day I took a walk in the country and I met a little farmer mouse in a red necktie. He thought he would like to live in town.

"Ough!" the Town Mouse shivers, "I wish I were safe in the country, now!"

There is a little noise at the back of the pantry, and the Country Mouse enters in great glee, looking about at all the food. The Cat sees the Country Mouse, and she creeps, softly, a little farther under the shelf, keeping watch of him all the time.

The Town Mouse, jumping down from the table, and motioning with one paw for the Country Mouse to make less noise:

"Oh, why did you come? It isn't safe here. You should have stayed in the country."

The Country Mouse, paying no attention to the Town Mouse, but running nimbly around the table and tasting all the different things.

The Country Mouse: "Cheese, and bread, and cake, and pie—and jam!"

He puts his paw down in a jam pot, and eats a little jam. Then he crosses to the Town Mouse and pats him on his back.

The Country Mouse: "A thousand thanks, my fine fellow. This pantry of yours is a palace, and you are the prince. No quiet, country life for me. Here will we live and eat our fill—"

He stops suddenly, as the Cat once more sneezes.

The Town Mouse, wringing his paws, and whispering in great fright: "I heard it a moment or so ago. I'll wager I heard it; and now I hear it again. Some one sneezed."

The Country Mouse, glancing about, but seeing no one: "Who sneezed?"

The Town Mouse: "The Cat."

The Country Mouse: "Where is the Cat?"

The Town Mouse: "The Cat is everywhere. She isn't in the room, now, but she may be on her way. Hours and hours she sits at the door of my hole so I can't come out in the evening. Then she chases me when I try to snatch a bite of supper, and she follows me—follows, wherever I go."

The Country Mouse, in a frightened voice: "Are her eyes as large as saucers? Does she wear cushions on her feet that no one may hear her when she walks? Has she sharp claws, and sharper teeth? Can she see in the dark? Does she eat—mice?"

The Cat suddenly springs from her corner. There is a great scamper, in which the mice make their escape, but the Country Mouse leaves his long tail in the Cat's paws.

Dramatic form arranged by Carolyn Sherwin Bailey.

STORIES SELECTED BECAUSE OF THEIR DRAMATIC
QUALITIES

JACK AND THE BEANSTALK	*Old Fairy Tale*
LITTLE RED RIDING HOOD	*Old Fairy Tale*
BRE'R RABBIT AND THE LITTLE TAR BABY	
Joel Chandler Harris, in Nights with Uncle Remus	
THE LARK AND HER YOUNG ONES	*Æsop's Fables*
THE LION AND THE MOUSE	*Æsop's Fables*
HANSEL AND GRETEL	*Old Fairy Tale*
THE PROUD CHICKEN	*Chinese Fable, in The Talking Beasts*

CHAPTER IX

STORY TELLING AN AID TO VERBAL EXPRESSION

NEARLY all children find fluent speech as readily as birds find song and flowers find perfume. Occasionally, there is a "different" child, though, who through shyness, slow motor reaction or a retarded brain development has difficulty in using words as a medium of expressing himself.

There is always the problem, too, of the foreign-born child. We find him a patient, tongue-tied little scrap of humanity clad in the garb of Italy or Russia or Germany clinging to his mother's skirts when the big vessel docks and as dazed as she is at the babel of strange speech that deafens, stuns him. Then we see him in school and his linguistic problem becomes more complicated. He is put into a class where the ordinarily complex matters of reading, writing, and ciphering are made increasingly more complex because they are presented to him in a foreign language. The school curriculum leaves small space in the day for teaching a child to talk. Tony, discouraged, baffled, puzzled, drifts farther and farther into his great silence and is dubbed a dunce, because he doesn't know what his teacher is talking about.

What shall we do with Tony who forms a big unit in our ever increasing foreign population? How shall we quickest help him and every child to that ready expression through speech that means power, efficiency, self-control in later years?

There was my own, special Tony—a quaint little man of five in yellow breeches, a green shirt and a fur cap, which latter he persisted in wearing during his entire school day for fear that some one might steal it. Tony was, "out of Naples." His melting brown eyes danced with delight at a bit of crimson paper, a gold orange produced as a model for the painting lesson, a red rose that meant a sense game. But Tony's warm, red lips remained persistently closed. Days melted into weeks and then were months and still Tony was dumb. Ideas he had. Words he had not, although I had tried daily to teach him to say, *good morning, good-by, ball, clay, blocks* and like words.

One day Tony electrified me, though. He was always an attentive, close listener during my story hour that ended the morning. Because the children were, in the majority, foreign, I selected short, repetitional stories for telling. The children were fascinated with the quaint old folk tale of "The Teeny Tiny Lady." As I told it, they had formed a habit of joining me when I reached a familiar phrase.

"Tell the Teeny Tiny Lady," they begged again and as I finished the story, Tony's eyes danced, his lips parted—

"Once upon a time there was a lady, who lived in a house in a village," he began in clear, pure English. With a little help he almost retold the story. It was amazing, but through the inspiration of the other children's enthusiastic story interest, the many repetitions of the story and its simple, cumulative structure Tony had learned nearly a hundred words. He talked after that, and he told us stories. The story had unloosed his tongue.

Stories help children to verbal expression.

In the case of a foreign child who must be taught English, or the American-born child who is shy and so lacking in the power of expressing himself through words, we will use the old folk tale that repeats its words and phrasing with happy familiarity and so teaches speech.

It will not be necessary to make the child or group of children feel that the story is being used as a lesson in English.

Just select the *right story.*

Tell it *over and over again,* as long as the children are interested in it—and you will find that their interest will exhaust yours.

And encourage the children to *tell the story with you.*

This method spells success in using the story to increase a child's vocabulary.

Certain stories stimulate the child to repeat certain jingles or phrases *with* the story teller. This explains their popularity and adds to

174

their value. The good old cumulative story of the "Cat and the Mouse" is built around a nonsense ditty:

"First she leaped, and then she ran,
'Till she came to the cow and thus began."

After a child learns and repeats this verse he begins to add to it the sentences of the story that precede and follow it. When the foreign child is able to tell the last paragraph of the story:—

"So the good baker gave the mouse some bread; the mouse gave the bread to the butcher who gave him some meat; the mouse gave the meat to the farmer who gave him an armful of hay; the mouse gave the hay to the cow and the cow gave the mouse a saucer of milk for the cat. Then the cat drank the milk and gave the mouse his little long tail. And they went on playing in the malt house."

—he has acquired a good working vocabulary of English.

So there are a score of similar repetitional stories that help a child to learn ready speech. The Greedy Cat repeats the tale of his prowess:

"I have eaten my friend the mouse. I have eaten an old woman, and a man and a donkey, and the King and all his elephants. What is to . hinder my eating you, too?"

Chicken Little bewails to every one she meets:

"The sky is falling."

And in answer to the query "How do you know?" she assures her questioner:

"I saw it with my eyes, I heard it with my ears, and a bit of it fell upon my tail."

In Maud Lindsay's story of "The Little Gray Pony" there is a delightfully interpolated jingle that repeats itself and adds to itself in such fascinating fashion that children cannot resist saying with the story teller:

"Storekeeper! Storekeeper! I've come to you;
My little gray pony has lost his shoe!
And I want some coal the iron to heat,
That the blacksmith may shoe my pony's feet."

and its answer:

176

"Now, I have apples and candy to sell,
And more nice things than I can tell;
But I've no coal the iron to heat,
That the blacksmith may shoe your pony's feet."

Ever popular Little Half Chick with his happy-go-lucky, daring journey to Madrid compels children to tell his story as he *"hoppity kicks"* through his adventures. The Three Pigs with their three ever interesting fates help a child to do his own story telling. There is an exhaustless fund of folk lore to draw upon that has few words in its story construction, frequent and happy repetitions of those words, and inspiration for a child to make those words a part of his own vocabulary.

These bits of repeated phrasing in a story, scraps of incorporated lyrics and jingles and built-up cumulative paragraphs are like the beads that help to make the child's necklace. On them he strings the thread of the story narrative, making it so thoroughly a part of his mental life that he is able to give it out again in the remembered words of the story. Long after the loved, "huffing and puffing" of the wolf in the story of the "Three Little Pigs" has become only a memory, a child uses the words, *furze, blazing, scramble, fortune*—and a hundred other words that came to him in this happy story connection and so into his everyday conversation.

The older child who has passed the nursery tale and folk lore turnstile in his story road finds help to a greater power in verbal expression by means of the beautifully written story, told in its original pure phrasing by the story teller and enriching him because of its wonderful English. A truly well-wrought story suffers often at the hands of the story teller. It isn't necessary in telling such a story to bring it down to the plane of the children's intelligence; rather we will bring the children up to its heights of beautiful imagery and mellow phrasing.

In telling Henry Ward Beecher's story of "The Anxious Leaf," in "Norwood," the story should be memorized by the story teller. No word of its vivid picturing should be lost. It is a short story so this method of preparing it for telling will not be irksome. A little girl six years old who had been told this story several times was out walking one fall with her mother. She picked up a dead leaf, from the ground, and holding it tenderly in her hand, she repeated softly:

"Then the little leaf began to *want* to go and it grew very beautiful in thinking about it.

"And a little puff of wind came and tossed it like a spark of fire in the air and it fell gently down under the edge of the fence among hundreds of other leaves; and it fell into a dream and never waked up to tell what it dreamed about—"

This child's vocabulary had been deeply enriched by a story.

In Laura Richards' stories we find pure English that will help children. In Rudyard Kipling's "Jungle Stories" and the "Just So Stories" there is virile wording that every child needs. Dean Hodges' "Bible Stories" preserve for children the line phrasing of the Hebrews as almost no other Bible story teller has succeeded in doing. Hans Christian Andersen's best translators have kept for us his matchless word painting. Such stories as these teach a child purer use of English. Eugene Field's few child stories; "The Legend of Claus," "The Mouse and the Moonbeam," "The Maple Leaf and the Violet" sing in their classic wording. No child can hear them without having his vocabulary enriched.

It is quite possible to accomplish a great deal through story telling, not only in teaching English to the child who is foreign born or dormant mentally, but in giving the average child new and more colorful examples of word painting than he has heard before.

The steps in story telling for verbal expression in children are:

Selection. The story must be worth while telling from the point of view of its phrasing. In the case of the child who really needs to be taught to talk, short, rhymed or cumulative tales are useful. With older children we will select those beautiful examples of classic story telling that should form part of a child's mental life and so help him to express himself in pure diction.

Presentation. These stories that are se-

180

lected by the story teller as being particularly adapted to English teaching should be most carefully prepared and presented happily, compellingly, and in their exact, original form with almost no variation in subsequent telling so that they may present good models to the children.

Repetition. A story selected for its English value should have frequent repetitions that the children may become very familiar with it and gain the power to repeat it themselves, or at least learn certain parts of it, not as a task but naturally, inspirationally.

STORIES THAT HELP A CHILD TO VERBAL EXPRESSION

THE WOODPECKER WHO WAS SELFISH

There was once a little Lady Woodpecker— such a trim, tidy little Lady Woodpecker—who wore always a natty red bonnet, and a white apron and who lived in a hole in a big Pine Tree. Her house was cozy and comfortable, all lined with moss and wool, and protected by a little brown bark door so that it was cool in the summer time and warm when the winter winds blew.

But the little Lady Woodpecker was a selfish bird and she never, *never* asked any other birds to come and visit with her in her house in the Pine Tree.

In the next tree to the little Lady Woodpecker lived a Fluffy Sparrow. His nest was loosely built and untidy and it rested insecurely in a fork of a tree so that the wind blew it this way and that way. This was because all sparrows are poor nest builders and it was not the Fluffy Sparrow's fault at all. One day there was an unusually heavy storm and down from the tree blew the nest. So the Sparrow had now no home.

Then the Fluffy Sparrow flew and hopped and twittered beside the little brown bark door above the little Lady Woodpecker and said:

"Oh, little Lady Woodpecker with the red bonnet, have pity on me and take me into your house, for the rain falls and I am very, very cold."

But the little Lady Woodpecker tapped with her bill on the wall of her house and answered:

"I can't let you in to-day, Fluffy Sparrow. I am cooking juniper berries for a batch of pies. Come again some other time and perhaps I will let you in."

So the Fluffy Sparrow hopped away and the rain made him very, **very** cold.

The next day the Fluffy Sparrow flew and hopped and twittered again beside the little brown bark door of the little Lady Woodpecker and said:

"Oh, little Lady Woodpecker with the red bonnet, have pity on me and take me into your house, for the cold and cruel wind blows and it ruffles my feathers."

But the little Lady Woodpecker tapped again with her bill on the wall of her house and answered:

"I can't let you in to-day, Fluffy Sparrow. I am washing the pot in which I cooked a batch of juniper berries for a batch of pies. Come again some other time and perhaps I will let you in."

So the Fluffy Sparrow hopped away and the cold and cruel wind ruffled his feathers.

The day after that the Fluffy Sparrow flew and hopped and twittered again beside the little brown bark door of the little Lady Woodpecker and said:

"Oh, little Lady Woodpecker, have pity on me and take me into your house, for the biting frost nips my feet."

But the little Lady Woodpecker tapped again with her bill on the wall of her house and answered:

"I can't let you in to-day, Fluffy Sparrow. I am making the crust for my batch of juniper berry pies. Come again some other time and perhaps I will let you in."

So the Fluffy Sparrow hopped away and the biting frost nipped his feet.

But the fourth day the Fluffy Sparrow flew and hopped and twittered once again beside the little brown bark door of the little Lady Woodpecker and said:

"Oh, little Lady Woodpecker with the little red bonnet, have pity on me and take me into your house, for the snow blinds me."

But the little Lady Woodpecker tapped *very* hard with her bill on the wall of her house and answered:

"I can't let you in to-day, Fluffy Sparrow. I am cleaning my floor before I sit down, all by myself, to *eat* my juniper berry pies."

So the blinding frost blinded the Fluffy Sparrow's eyes.

Then the last day of all the Fluffy Sparrow flew and hopped and twittered beside the little brown bark door of the little Lady Woodpecker and he said:

"Oh, little Lady Woodpecker with the little red bonnet, *please* have pity on me and take me into your house, for I do not like the rain and the wind and the frost and the snow."

184

But the little Lady Woodpecker did not answer the Fluffy Sparrow. And the Fluffy Sparrow lifted one claw and poked open the little bark door and he saw that *no one was inside.* The little Lady Woodpecker was away buying a key with which to lock her door while she ate her batch of juniper berry pies.

So the Fluffy Sparrow went inside the house in the tree that was so cozy and comfortable because it was lined with moss and wool. There he was sheltered from the rain and the wind and the frost and the snow. He ate up all the batch of juniper berry pies.

When the little Lady Woodpecker came home the Fluffy Sparrow was living in *her* house and she had to find herself a new one because she had been such a selfish bird.

An Indian Folk Tale.

THE LITTLE RABBIT WHO WANTED RED WINGS

Once upon a time there was a little White Rabbit with two beautiful long pink ears and two bright red eyes and four soft little feet—*such* a pretty little White Rabbit, but he wasn't happy.

Just think, this little White Rabbit wanted to

185

be somebody else instead of the nice little rabbit that he was.

When Mr. Bushy Tail, the gray squirrel, went by, the little White Rabbit would say to his Mammy:

"Oh, Mammy, I *wish* I had a long gray tail like Mr. Bushy Tail's."

And when Mr. Porcupine went by, the little White Rabbit would say to his Mammy:

"Oh, Mammy, I *wish* I had a back full of bristles like Mr. Porcupine's."

And when Miss Puddle-Duck went by in her two little red rubbers, the little White Rabbit would say:

" Oh, Mammy, I *wish* I had a pair of red rubbers like Miss Puddle-Duck's."

So he went on and on wishing until his Mammy was clean tired out with his wishing and Old Mr. Ground Hog heard him one day.

Old Mr. Ground Hog is very wise indeed, so he said to the little White Rabbit:

"Why don't you-all go down to Wishing Pond, and if you look in the water at yourself and turn around three times in a circle, you-all will get your wish."

So the little White Rabbit trotted off, all alone

by himself through the woods until he came to a little pool of green water lying in a low tree stump, and that was the Wishing Pond. There was a little, *little* bird, all red, sitting on the edge of the Wishing Pond to get a drink, and as soon as the little White Rabbit saw him he began to wish again:

"Oh, I wish I had a pair of little red wings!" he said. Just then he looked in the Wishing Pond and he saw his little white face. Then he turned around three times and something happened. He began to have a queer feeling in his shoulders, like he felt in his mouth when he was cutting his teeth. It was his wings coming through. So he sat all day in the woods by the Wishing Pond waiting for them to grow, and, by and by, when it was almost sundown, he started home to see his Mammy and show her, because he had a beautiful pair of long, trailing red wings.

But by the time he reached home it was getting dark, and when he went in the hole at the foot of a big tree where he lived, his Mammy didn't know him. No, she really and truly did not know him, because, you see, she had never seen a rabbit with red wings in all her life. And so the little White Rabbit had to go out again, because his Mammy

187

wouldn't let him get into his own bed. He had to go out and look for some place to sleep all night.

He went and went until he came to Mr. Bushy Tail's house, and he rapped on the door and said:

"Please, kind Mr. Bushy Tail, may I sleep in your house all night?"

But Mr. Bushy Tail opened his door a crack and then he slammed it tight shut again. You see he had never seen a rabbit with red wings in all his life.

So the little White Rabbit went and went until he came to Miss Puddle-Duck's nest down by the marsh and he said:

"Please, kind Miss Puddle-Duck, may I sleep in your nest all night?"

But Miss Puddle-Duck poked her head up out of her nest just a little way and then she shut her eyes and stretched her wings out so far that she covered her whole nest.

You see she had never seen a rabbit with red wings in all her life.

So the little White Rabbit went and went until he came to Old Mr. Ground Hog's hole and Old Mr. Ground Hog let him sleep with him all night, but the hole had beech nuts spread all over it. Old Mr. Ground Hog liked to sleep on them, but they hurt the little White Rabbit's feet and made him very uncomfortable before morning.

When it came morning, the little White Rabbit decided to try his wings and fly a little, so he climbed up on a hill and spread his wings and sailed off, but he landed in a low bush all full of prickles, and his four feet got mixed up with the twigs so he couldn't get down.

"Mammy, Mammy, Mammy, come and help me!" he called.

His Mammy didn't hear him, but Old Mr. Ground Hog did, and he came and helped the little White Rabbit out of the prickly bush.

"Don't you-all want your red wings?" Mr. Ground Hog asked.

"No, *no!*" said the little White Rabbit.

"Well," said the Old Ground Hog, "why don't you-all go down to the Wishing Pond and wish them *off* again?"

So the little White Rabbit went down to the Wishing Pond and he saw his face in it. Then he turned around three times, and, sure enough, his red wings were gone. Then he went home to his Mammy, who knew him right away and was so glad to see him and he never, *never* wished to be something different from what he really was again.

Southern Folk Tale.

FOR THE STORY TELLER

STORIES SELECTED BECAUSE OF THEIR STIMULUS
TO VERBAL EXPRESSION IN CHILDREN

THE CAT AND THE MOUSE *In Firelight Stories*
THE LITTLE GRAY PONY *Maud Lindsay, in Mother Stories*
THE LITTLE BOY WHO FOUND HIS FORTUNE *In Firelight Stories*
THE STORY OF IBBITY *In Firelight Stories*
THE CAT, THE COCK AND THE FOX
Kate Douglas Wiggin, in Tales of Laughter
TOM TIT TOT *Kate Douglas Wiggin, in Tales of Laughter*
THE LITTLE PINK ROSE
Sara Cone Bryant, in Best Stories to Tell to Children
THE LITTLE TRAVELER *Maud Lindsay, in Mother Stories*
TOM, THE WATER BABY
Charles Kingsley, adapted in For the Children's Hour

CHAPTER X

A GROUP of school children recently started quarreling in the school yard during the morning recess time. The storm center was two small boys who had fallen out over a game of marbles. The entire class took sides; *for* Edgar and *against* Edgar, *for* Lawrence and *against* Lawrence and proceeded to wage individual warfare like a miniature army. Even the ringing of the school bell failed to stop the quarrel. The children took their seats unwillingly and with sour faces carrying the feud with them into the classroom.

The teacher was a wise young person who believed in attacking the matter of discipline along the lines of least resistance. She saw immediately that a general feeling of anger possessed the children; no one child could be blamed. So she set about creating an opposite, general feeling as quickly as possible. Setting aside other work for ten minutes she announced a story. Instantly, the tension was loosened. By the time she had finished Grimm's story of "The Pot and the Kettle," in which, as a climax, neither is able to taunt the other with being black, the children's anger was gone, peace was restored, and the children were smiling. An emotional crisis had been successfully met by means of a story.

Our emotions, that is, our feelings of anger, joy, sorrow, hatred, jealousy, and love are older than we are. They may almost be classed as instinctive, for they manifest themselves so early. The baby gives examples of emotional explosions in his first month. These feelings have their rise in mental conditions over which we have no control; they are not dependent upon sensory stimuli; they are isolated, incoherent. They take hold of the personality of the subject in a hypnotic fashion, for the period of the feeling's mastery we *are* anger, love, sorrow, or whatever emotion enthralls us.

The psychologists classify and subdivide the emotions into many divisions but the story teller is most concerned with making one elastic, wide classification of a child's emotions; those that are concerned with *bodily expression.* A child is happy, he laughs; he is sad and he cries; he is angry, he fights; he is afraid, and he gives active evidence of cowardice. Because, during the time of his obsession by one of these emotions, a child is so completely mastered by his feelings, we discover that we can create for him by story suggestion a similar mental state.

The story which a child feels is going to be a force in his emotional development.

I came across one of my own, old Mother Goose books not long ago with the leaves that held the story of the "Babes in the Wood" *pinned* securely together. It told me as nothing else could have done the emotion caused in a child's mind by this gruesome tale. I was afraid when I read the story. I felt all the terror experienced by the Babes in the Wood. My fear emotion was so unpleasant that I had pinned the story out of my sight.

I wanted to feel some other emotion. Other children have similar emotions.

We will study stories, then, asking ourselves:

What emotion does this story stimulate?

By its unpleasant situations and images, does it inspire fear in a child? Does it make a child happy because of its bubbling good humor? Does it create child sympathy, courage, grief, anger, malice, charity, temperance? Each one of these states of feeling is characterized by bodily expression and we can almost mold character, and influence a child's future life activity by means of the stories which we tell him.

Sometimes our sole object in this story emotion work will be to create an atmosphere of good humor and happiness in our children. Not by any means to be despised is the ability to make a child laugh. The power to feel humor in childhood means the power to take life not too seriously in adult life and the story that simply amuses and entertains has an important place in the story hour. In this class of happiness-making stories are: "Bre'r Rabbit and the Little Tar Baby," "Johnny Cake," "Epaminondos and His Aunty," "The Mouse and the Sausage," "The Greedy Cat," "Lambikin," "Chicken Little," "The Cat and the Mouse" and a score more of sheer nonsense stories whose very improbability makes them tickle a child's sense of humor and gives him the opportunity to express his feelings in laughter.

So many more stories than we realize put children into a state of fear. Oldest of all our emotions, since we share it alike with animals, fear peculiarly takes hold of a child during the early years when he is most interested in stories. The story situation that seems quite plausible to us and not in the least terrorizing, haunts a child at night, peers from shadowy corners at him in the daytime and makes of him, unwittingly, a little coward. The troll with only one eye, the giant who cracks human bones, the witch who exercises horrible spells should all be buried in some tomb of forgetfulness. Stories having such themes do nothing toward creating worthwhile emotions in the child's mind. While their very improbability makes them plausible for us, they are, on the other hand, very real to children and should be avoided.

But we can make children self reliant and brave by giving them feelings of courage through listening to courage stories. The child who hears the stories of "Cedric, the Little Hero of Harlem," "The Story of a Short Life," "David and Goliath," "Jean D'Arc," "Tiny Tim," "Jenny Wren," is made one with each child hero, feels with them, dares with them, acts with them.

Each emotion that will prevail over and influence human action in adult life may be appealed to in childhood through stories.

The child who is greedy and selfish is led into a better state of feeling when he hears the story of "The King of the Golden River." Always greed and avarice will be associated in his mind with the tragic end of the brothers, and the Happy Valley, full of plenty, and enjoyed by Gluck, will symbolize for him the reward of unselfishness. The child who is proud will feel the opposite emotion, humbleness, when he hears Oscar Wilde's wonderful parable of "The Star-Child." As children follow the wanderings of the Star-Child, his beauty gone, his mother lost to him because of his pride and, with him, find the successful end of the journey, they lose their own pride of heart with their story hero.

"And the gate of the palace opened, and the priests and the high officers of the city ran forth to meet him, and they abased themselves before him, and said, 'Thou art our lord for whom we have been waiting, and the son of our King.'

"And the Star-Child answered them and said, 'I am no king's son, but the child of a poor beggar-woman. And how say ye that I am beautiful, for I know that I am evil to look at.'

"Then he, whose armour was inlaid with gilt flowers, and on whose helmet couched a lion that had wings, held up a shield, and cried, 'How saith my lord that he is not beautiful?'

"And the Star-Child looked, and lo! his face was even as it had been, and his comeliness had come back to him, and he saw that in his eyes which he had not seen there before.

"And the priests and the high officers knelt down and said to him, 'It was prophesied of old that on this day should come he who was to rule

over us. Therefore, let our lord take this crown
and this sceptre, and be in his justice and mercy
our King over us.'

"But he said to them, 'I am not worthy, for I
have denied the mother who bare me, nor may I
rest till I have found her, and known her forgiveness. Therefore, let me go, for I must wander
again over the world, and may not tarry here,
though ye bring me the crown and the sceptre.'
And as he spake he turned his face from them
towards the street that led to the gate of the city,
and lo! amongst the crowd that pressed round
the soldiers, he saw the beggar-woman who was
his mother, and at her side stood the leper, who
had sat by the road.

"And a cry of joy broke from his lips, and he
ran over, and kneeling down he kissed the wounds
on his mother's feet, and wet them with his tears.
He bowed his head in the dust, and sobbing, as
one whose heart might break, he said to her:
'Mother, I denied thee in the hour of my pride.
Accept me in the hour of my humility. Mother,
I gave thee hatred. Do thou give me love.
Mother, I rejected thee. Receive thy child
now.' But the beggar-woman answered him not
a word.

"And he reached out his hands, and clasped

198

the white feet of the leper, and said to him: 'Thrice did I give thee of my mercy. Bid my mother speak to me once.' But the leper answered him not a word.

"And he sobbed again, and said: 'Mother, my suffering is greater than I can bear. Give me thy forgiveness, and let me go back to the forest.' And the beggar-woman put her hand on his head, and said to him: 'Rise,' and the leper put his hand on his head, and said to him 'Rise,' also.

"And he rose up from his feet, and looked at them, and lo! they were a King and a Queen.

"And the Queen said to him, 'This is thy father whom thou hast succored.'

"And the King said, 'This is thy mother whose feet thou hast washed with thy tears.'

"And they fell on his neck and kissed him, and brought him into the palace, and clothed him in fair raiment, and set the crown upon his head, and the sceptre in his hand, and over the city that stood by the river he ruled, and was its lord. Much justice and mercy did he show to all, and the evil Magician he banished, and to the Woodcutter and his wife he sent many rich gifts, and to their children he gave high honour. Nor would he suffer any to be cruel to bird or beast, but taught love and loving-kindness and charity, and to the poor he gave bread, and to the naked he gave raiment, and there was peace and plenty in the land."

What more effective emotional stimulus could be found than this?

The children whom we wish to feel pity should hear Andersen's "Ugly Duckling"; Oscar Wilde's, "The Birthday of the Infanta"; Daudet's, "The Last Lesson"; "The House in the Wood" and "The Star Dollars" by Grimm and many other *sympathy* stories that only wait for our timely rendering.

In telling a story, having in mind its emotional effect upon a child's mental life, we will need to use the greatest delicacy of discrimination in order to create just the story effect which we wish. We will not tell such stories so often as to cause them to lose their magic spell. We will appeal to but one emotion at a time through the story medium. We will make an appeal most strongly to those emotions that have bodily expression in a child's daily speech and acts. We will remember that a child is so quick to smiles, so quick to tears that the pleasanter feelings should be the aim of our telling of emotion stories rather than the unpleasant ones.

Some of us may class Miss Mulock's story of "The Little Lame Prince" as just a purely imaginative one; others of us are appealed to by its dramatic qualities. But, after all, the story has survived the test of years because of its big emotional appeal. It stands for pity, sympathy, courage, nearly all the emotions which we wish to strengthen in children.

THE LITTLE LAME PRINCE

Yes, he was the most beautiful Prince that ever was born. Everybody was exceedingly proud of him, especially his father and mother, the King and Queen of Nomansland. The only person who did not love the Prince was the King's brother, who would have been king one day if the royal baby had not come.

Of course a little Prince must be christened. The day came at last, as lovely as the Prince himself, and they carried the baby, magnificent in his christening robe, to the bedside of the Queen, his mother. She admired him very much. She kissed and blessed him, and then she gave him up with a gentle smile, and turned peacefully over in her bed, saying nothing more to anybody.

It was a wonderful christening procession: dukes and duchesses, princes and princesses, heralds, and ladies in waiting were in line. Every one was so busy shouting out the little Prince's four and twenty names that they never noticed the accident. It was the Prince's state nurse maid, an elegant young lady of rank, who let him fall just at the foot of the marble staircase. She had been so busy arranging her train—that was the reason she dropped him—but she contrived to pick him up again the next minute before any one saw. The baby had turned very pale under the heap of lace and muslin, and he had moaned a little, but that was all.

There were pages in crimson and gold, troops of little girls in dazzling white with baskets of flowers, the King and his train on one side—as pretty a sight as ever was seen out of fairyland.

"The only thing the baby wants is a fairy godmother," said one of the children.

"Does he?" said a shrill, but soft voice behind.

She was no bigger than a child, and certainly had not been invited to the christening. She was a little old woman dressed all in gray; gray gown, gray hooded cloak of a material tinted like the gray of an evening sky, gray hair, and her eyes were gray also. Even her face had a soft gray shadow over it, but she was not unpleasantly old, and her smile was as sweet and childlike as the Prince's own.

"Take care," she said. "Don't let the baby fall again!"

The grand lady nurse started.

"Who spoke? His Royal Highness is just going to sleep," she said.

"Nevertheless I must kiss him," said the little old woman. "I am his godmother."

And she stretched herself up on tiptoe, and gave the little Prince three kisses.

"An insult to His Royal Highness," said the nurse.

"His Majesty shall hear of this," said a lord-in-waiting. But just then the little gray woman faded away like air, and the great bell of the palace —the bell which was only heard on the death of some member of the Royal family—began to toll —one—two—three—nine and twenty—just the Queen's age!

So when the little Prince was carried back to his mother's room, there was no mother to kiss him. She had turned her face to the window whence one could just see the Beautiful Mountains where she was born. So gazing, she had quietly died.

Everybody was very kind to the poor little
Prince, but, somehow, after his mother died, things
seemed to go wrong with him. From a beautiful
baby he became sickly and pale, and his legs, which
had been so fat and strong, withered and shrank.
When he tried to stand he only tumbled down.

A prince, and not able to walk! People began
to say what a misfortune it was to the country.
Rather a misfortune to him, also, poor little lad,
but he still had the old sweet look in his little face,
and his body grew if his legs did not. His Majesty, the King, took very little notice of his son,
and one day he died, too, and they made the
Crown Prince, Regent, in his stead, and then
things went much worse with the little Prince.

Perhaps the Prince Regent did not mean to do
wrong. He told the country that the little Prince
would be better if he were sent for a while to the
Beautiful Mountains. So the poor little Prince
started, with two whole regiments to guard him,
and then there came back word that he had gone
on a much longer journey. They said that he had
died on the road, so the country went into mourn-
ing, and then forgot all about their little lame
Prince. And the Regent was proclaimed King.

What really became of the Prince? Beyond
the Mountains there lay a barren tract of country,

with not a bush—not a tree. In summer the sunshine fell upon it hour after hour, and in winter the snow covered it steadily and noiselessly in one great sheet. Not a pleasant place to live—and no one did live there, evidently. The only human habitation for miles and miles was one large, round stone tower, circular, with neither doors nor windows, save some slits in the wall near the top. And the top was a hundred feet from the plain.

One winter night, when all the plain was white with moonlight, there was seen crossing it a great black horse, ridden by a man equally black, and carrying before him on the saddle a woman and a child. The woman had a sad, fierce look, and no wonder, for she was a criminal under sentence of death, but her sentence had been changed. She was to live in the lonely tower with a child—only as long as he lived. He was a little gentle boy, with a sweet, sleepy smile. He had been tired with his long journey. And he was very helpless, with his poor, small, shrivelled legs, which could neither stand nor run away—for the little boy was the Prince.

When they reached the foot of the tower there was light enough to see a huge chain dangling from the top, half way. The man fitted together a ladder and mounted, drawing up the Prince and his nurse. Then he came down again and left them alone.

And there they stayed for years.

It was not an unhappy life for the little boy. He had all sorts and kinds of beautiful toys, and more picture books than he could look at. He learned to crawl like a fly, and to jump like a frog. He played about from room to room—there were four; parlor, kitchen, his nurse's room, and his own—and as he grew older he would sit at the slits of windows and watch the sky, and wonder about things—for his nurse never talked much.

"I wish I had somebody to tell me all about the world," he said to himself once, "a real, live person. Oh, I want somebody dreadfully!"

As he spoke, there sounded behind him, the tap-tap-tap of a cane, and—what do you think he saw?

A little woman, no larger than he, with gray hair, and a dress of gray, and there was a gray shadow over her wherever she moved. But she had the sweetest smile, and the prettiest hands, which she laid on his shoulders, as she said:

"My own little boy, I couldn't come until you said you wanted me, but here I am!"

"Are you my mother?" asked the little Prince. He had always wondered what had become of his mother.

"No, only your godmother," said the little woman, "but I love you as much as your mother did, and I want to help you all I can, my poor little boy. I am going to give you a present—a traveling cloak," but just then in came the Prince's nurse, and his lovely old godmother melted away, as a rainbow melts out of the sky. He knew, for he had watched one many a time.

And what of the traveling cloak? I will tell you all about it.

It was the commonest-looking bundle imaginable —shabby and small. It seemed no treasure at all; only a circular, green piece of cloth, and quite worn and shabby. It had a slit cut to the center, forming a round hole for the neck, and that was all its shape.

"Of what use will it be to me?" thought the little Prince sadly. "I never go out. She must be a rather funny person, this dear old godmother of mine."

But he spread it out on the floor, and sat down in the center for all the world like a frog on a water lily leaf. The edges of the cloak began turning up—and—the cloak rose, slowly and steadily, and higher and higher until the little Prince was obliged to open the skylight to let himself through. There they were outside.

Oh, it was wonderful, nothing but earth and sky for a while. Then came the patches of flowers that grew on the plain, white saxifrage, and yellow lotus, and ground thistles. Next, he saw a farm where cows and horses, lambs and sheep fed in the meadows. Presently he heard a murmur in the distance, like a gigantic hive of bees. It was a great city which he was sailing over and the cloak stopped directly over a palace.

Such a magnificent palace! It had terraces and gardens, battlements and towers. Its windows looked in all directions, but mostly toward the Beautiful Mountains.

"I wonder if there is a king in this palace," thought the little Prince.

Just then the cloak settled down to the palace roof between some great stacks of chimneys as comfortably as if it were on the ground. There were some broken tiles in the roof, and the Prince peered in.

It was the largest room he had ever seen, and very grand. There was the loveliest carpet ever woven on the floor, a bed of flowers; but the room was perfectly empty and silent. In the center of a magnificent bed, large enough to hold six people, lay a small figure, something like wax work, fast asleep—very fast asleep. There were some sparkling rings on the fingers and the nose was sharp and thin, and a long gray beard lay over the breast. Two little flies buzzed about the curtains of the bed, and made the only sound—for the King was dead.

Then there came a great shouting from the city.

"Long live the King! The King is dead— down with the King! Hurrah for the Republic! Hurrah for no government at all!"

"Oh, dear godmother," cried the little Prince. "Let me go back to the tower." And he suddenly found himself in his own room alone and quiet— for the traveling cloak had taken him there; after which it folded itself into the tiniest bundle, and tied its own knots, and rolled itself into the farthest and darkest corner.

The clock was striking ten, and no nurse was to be seen. The little lame Prince crawled about from room to room on his weak little knees, but all the four chambers were deserted.

"Nurse—dear nurse—please come back!" he cried. "Come back and I will be the best boy in the land!"

But she did not answer, nor come.

In truth the poor woman had not been such a wicked woman after all. As soon as she heard of the death of the King, she determined to go to

Nomansland, and set upon the throne its rightful heir. She had persuaded the old black messenger to take her down from the tower, and together they galloped like the wind from city to city spreading the news that the little lame Prince was alive and well, and the noblest young Prince that ever was born.

It was a bold stroke, but it succeeded.

"Hurrah for the Prince! Let the little Prince be our King," came from end to end of the Kingdom.

Everybody tried to remember what a dear baby he once was, and nobody at all spoke of his lameness. They went with great rejoicing; lords and gentlemen, and soldiers traveling night and day to fetch the little lame Prince.

They found him sitting on the floor—quite pale, for he expected a far different end from this, although he had decided to die, if die he must, courageously, like a Prince.

"Yes," he said, "I am only a little boy, but I will try to be your King. I will do my best to make the people happy."

Then there arose from inside and outside the tower, such a shout as never yet was heard across the lonely plain.

So the little lame Prince came to his own after

all, and every one says he was the best King that ever ruled Nomansland. His reign lasted for years and years, and then he went away.

Whither he went, or who went with him, it is impossible to say. But I myself believe that his godmother took him on his traveling cloak to the Beautiful Mountains. What he did there, or where he is now, who can tell? I cannot. But one thing I am quite sure of, that, wherever he is, he is perfectly happy.

And so, when I think of him, am I.

Adapted from Miss Mulock.

STORIES SELECTED BECAUSE OF A SPECIAL EMOTIONAL APPEAL IN EACH

CHAPTER XI

IMAGINATION AND THE FAIRY STORY

WHAT is child imagination?
The Puritans thought the imaginative person was a liar. Old Salem said that such a vision as is conjured into reality by the imagination constituted witchcraft. Even to-day there are parents and teachers who believe that the child who has the power to pierce the veil of reality and see into a beyond is a dreamer who lacks stability of mind and practicality of purpose. But the unexplainable power by means of which a human mind grasps a bundle of bare, dry facts, sorts them over speculatively and then pieces them together into a new, luminous bit of mind stuff, different from anything seen, or heard or handled by that personality before—this is the miracle working of what we know as constructive imagination. Edison chaining elec-

tricity and perpetuating the human voice imaged these wonders before he realized them. Moissant saw air craft through the telescope of his mind before he built bird machines. Jane Addams saw, felt, imaged herself alone, poor and an outcast before she could successfully help her fellows. In adult life, the power to image the unreal, the power to feel with another personality spells genius, as well as imagination.

Child imagination is a kaleidoscopic mind method of seeing, and piecing, and patching together ideas gathered by the senses, and making of them a new concept.

No child ever saw a live fairy, but any child will explain a fairy to you, quite plausibly, because he has formed his own fairy concept. A being with hair like his favorite small girl friend, and the stature of his little sister's doll, having wings like the dragon fly he saw last summer and dressed in something colored and soft and rustling like his mother's dresses, a person capable of doing all that the story books say she can do—this is a child's mind picture of a fairy.

No one of us ever saw Heaven but all of us can describe it. A place of this world's grass and flowers and music and familiar, beloved personalities transplanted, renewed, translated—this is our manner of describing, of seeing Heaven.

The child's method of imaging a fairy and our method of imaging Heaven are identical. From known, experienced, familiar perceptions we make a new, as yet unexperienced concept. If we want a child to see Heaven, we must help him to see fairies. Success, happiness, efficiency, belief—all these in adult life are dependent upon the proper stimulating of the child's constructive imagination.

A good fairy story is the best stimulus to child imagination.

Not *any* fairy story, selected with slight discrimination and told to a child just because it is a story of fancy, however. "Blue Beard," "Ali Baba," "The Cruel Stepmother" do little but cause child nightmares and give children ideas of cruelty, vengeance and crime. These concepts will present themselves to the child soon enough in the daily newspapers.

Let us shut them out of the story hour. In selecting a fairy story to tell to children, we will first analyze it with exceeding care, asking ourselves these questions in regard to it:

What constitutes the imaginative element of this story?

Is its point of unreality an idea which we want to give permanence in the child's mind?

Is the story told in a series of such familiar, known images that there is material in it for stimulating the child's constructive imagination?

If a fanciful story survives these three tests, we may be sure that it is perfect.

There is Hans Andersen's story of "The Faithful Tin Soldier." Its climax is told in a lesson of heroism and faithfulness, qualities that we wish to make permanent in the child's mind through the medium of the imagination. And how are these qualities presented? We find that they are made real to children by means of familiar settings; a little boy is playing with new toys upon his birthday, we see the child going to bed, there is the coming-alive of the toys in the play-room, the tin soldier's experiences in the street, his return to the kitchen. Every child knows toys, a birthday, a play-room, a city street in the rain, a kitchen; but out of these patches of gray, every-day pigment Andersen paints for children a new, colored picture of fancy. Presented in terms of the real we have the unreal; a live tin soldier who is as heroic and faithful as we wish our children to be. This is a perfect imaginative story, a bit of unreality which we wish to make real for children and told in terms of child experience.

Alice Brown's wonderful allegory, "The Gradual Fairy," is also perfect in its theme and construction. Its hero, the Green Goblin, wishes to become a fairy. The story of his changing his ugly colors for those of the flowers when he promises never to hurt them again, losing his harsh, shrill voice by being kind to the brook, and so gradually finding beauty, is a marvellously compelling bit of imagery to leave with a child and it is told in familiar, right-at-hand word pictures. In the several chapters of Jean Ingelow's, "Mopsa, the Fairy," child hearers are transported to familiar places, but places where the unusual, the beautiful happens. The story tells of the Winding Up Places where tired-out horses are put in green pastures and are allowed to grow back to colt-hood, and where weary working folks are wound up, like clocks, and given such vigor that they never run down again.

Charles Kingsley, from the reality of a dirty chimney sweep and a sooty chimney, takes children voyaging into his paradise of fancy under the sea. Eugene Field gives children a permanent picture of Santa Claus in his legend of "Claus." There is the little lad, Claus, up in the Northland, finding his greatest happiness in carving wooden dolls and animals for the children. When his parents disappear, Claus lights his father's forge fire and in the wonder light of the Northern star pledges himself to create child happiness. The elves bringing him gifts of metal and precious stones for his work, the forest giving him its trees and greens, the reindeer drawing his sleigh full of toys, the snow and frost speeding him on his way—these give children the true meaning of Claus' world saint-ship in terms of the imagination.

Apply this threefold test to every imaginative story and your selection will be infallible.

What does the story image?

Do I want to vivify this image for my children?

How does it stimulate the imagination?

The old, loved fairy stories that have lived for centuries stand this test. The story of Cinderella leaves a child with a mental picture of a cinder maid full blown into a princess but with this image is the lesson of rewarded faithfulness to duty, and the story plot is built up of familiar concepts; the kitchen, a pumpkin, a party, a chiming clock, a tiny slipper. "The House in the Wood," "Little Daylight," "The Many Furred Creature," "Snow White and Rose Red," "The Goose Girl," "Briar Rose," "Spindle, Needle and Shuttle," "The Elves and the Shoemaker," "The Story of Midas," "The Star Dollars," "Why the Sea is Salt," "Tom Thumb," all these world-old fanciful tales take children far afield but they leave them better off, ethically, than before they heard them and each story is a healthy stimulus to the imagination.

What is the place of the fairy story in the story hour?

A good fairy story is like the touch of spice that gives the needed zest to a dish, it is the sweet at the end of the meal, it should not be spoiled by over use, by voraciousness. We will select our fairy stories with the utmost care, measuring each by our threefold rule. We will tell these perfect fairy tales occasionally only, realizing that they will bear frequent retelling and are to be the classics of the child's story literature.

One of the most beautiful of all fairy stories, Mary Wilkins Freeman wrote. "The Blue Robin" is perfect in treatment and theme.

THE BLUE ROBIN

The country over which King Chrysanthemum reigned was very far inland, so there was very little talk about the sea-serpent, but everybody was agitated over the question whether there was, or was not, a Blue Robin.

The whole kingdom was divided about it. The

members of parliament were "F. B. R.," for Blue Robin or "A. B. R.," against Blue Robin. The ladies formed clubs to discuss the question, and sometimes talked whole afternoons about it, and the children even laid down their dolls, and their tops to search for the Blue Robin. Indeed, many children had to be kept tied to their mother's apron-strings all the time to prevent them from running away to a Blue Robin hunt. It was a very common thing to see ladies going to a Blue Robin club, with a child at each apron-string, pulling back and crying, "I want to go hunting the Blue Robin! I want to go hunting the Blue Robin!"

The country was agitated over this question for many years, then finally there were riots about it.

People had to lock themselves in their houses, and when the Blue Robin party was uppermost, paint blue robins on their front doors, and when it was not, wash them off. After the riots commenced, it was really almost all that people could do to paint blue robins on and wash them off, their front doors.

At last King Chrysanthemum had to take extreme measures. He decided to consult the Wise Man. A committee was chosen of eight F. B. R.'s, and eight A. B. R.'s, and a chairman, and they set out at once, marching four abreast, the chairman with his chair leading the way, to consult the Wise Man. He had to be found before he could be consulted, however, and that was a very difficult matter. The Wise Man considered it the height of folly to live like other people in a house immovably fixed upon one spot of ground, and therefore he always carried his house about with him, as a turtle carries his shell.

He had fashioned a little dwelling of cloth and steel ribs, something like an umbrella, which he strapped to himself, and lived in, traveling all over the country in pursuit of wisdom.

The committee marched a whole week, before they came upon the Wise Man one afternoon in a pasture where huckleberries grew. He was standing quite still when they approached and made their obeisances. The Chairman of the committee placed his chair, a rocking-chair with a red plush cushion, before the Wise Man, seated himself, and spoke. "All Hail, Wise Man!" said he in a loud voice.

The Wise Man's house had a little door in front like a coach door, and two tiny windows. One of the windows had the curtains drawn, but out of the other looked the Wise Man's calm blue right eye. There was so much wisdom in his two eyes that he knew people could not comprehend it, so he always curtained one window. The house was about one foot higher than his head, and reached to his ankles. They could see his feet in their leather sandals below it.

The Wise Man said not one word in response to the Chairman's salutation, only looked at him with his blue right eye. Then the Chairman laid the matter before the Wise Man and besought his aid in the terrible situation of the country. After the Chairman had ceased speaking there was a silence for half an hour. Not a sound was to be heard except the creaking of the Chairman's rocking-chair. Then the Wise Man cleared his throat. The committee leaned forward expectantly, but they had to wait another half hour before he spoke, and then it was not very satisfactory. "Ideas are not as thick as huckleberries in this pasture," was all he said.

The committee looked at one another, and nodded ruefully. It was quite true, but it did not help them in their dilemma. They waited another half hour; then the Wise Man began moving off across the pasture in his house.

"Oh, stop, stop!" cried the Chairman. "Stop, stop!" cried the committee. They all ran after him, and begged him not to go away until he had given them some useful advice.

"Offer a reward!" called out the Wise Man, as he scudded away.

"For what, for what!" cried the committee.

"For finding the Blue Robin," called out the Wise Man, and then a puff of wind caught his umbrella-like house, and he was lifted quite off his feet, and bobbed away out of sight over the huckleberry-bushes.

The committee hastened back to the city, and reported. Another special parliament was called, and the reward for finding the Blue Robin was offered. That was really a difficult matter, because the Princess Honey was only five years old, and the customary reward—her hand in marriage —could hardly be offered. However, it was stated that if the finder of the Blue Robin was of suitable age when the Princess was grown, she should be his bride; and furthermore that he and all his relatives should be pensioned for life and that he should be appointed Poet Laureate, and given a regiment, a steam yacht, a special train, and a pound of candy every day from the national candy mills. The offer was painted in blue letters on yellow paper, and pasted up all over the country, and then the search began in good earnest.

Business all over the kingdom was at a standstill. Nobody did anything but hunt the Blue Robin.

People ate nothing in those days but cornmeal pudding, hastily mixed and boiled. There was no bread baked, because all the bakers and all the housewives were out hunting the Blue Robin. The mothers untied the children from their apron-strings, and the schools were all closed, because it was agreed that finding the Blue Robin and establishing peace in the kingdom, was of more importance than books, and all the children who were old enough were out hunting—that is, all the children except Poppy.

It should be stated here that everybody in this country, with the exception of the Princess, had a flower-name. The Princess was so much sweeter, that only the inmost sweetness of all flowers was good enough for her name, and she was called Honey.

Poppy was about ten years old, and his father was an editor of a newspaper, and very poor. He could scarcely support his five children. His wife had died the year before, and he could not afford to hire a housekeeper.

So Poppy had to stay at home, and keep the house, and take care of his four young brothers and sisters, while his father was away editing, and he could not hunt the Blue Robin. It was a great cross to him, but he loved his little brothers and sisters, and he made the best of it.

After the search for the Blue Robin began, his father was much busier, and had often to be away all night, so Poppy had to rock and trot the twin babies, Pink and Phlox, and go without sleep, after working hard cooking and washing dishes and sewing all day. Poppy had to mend the children's clothes, and he was even trying to make some little frocks for Petunia and Portulacca. They were twins also, five years old.

As Poppy sat in the window and sewed, with his right foot rocking Pink's cradle, and his left foot rocking Phlox's, with Petunia and Portulacca sitting beside him on their little stools, he told them all he had ever heard about the wonderful Blue Robin.

"Nobody is even quite certain he has seen it, himself," said Poppy, "but he knows somebody else, who knows somebody else, who has; and if you ever could find the first somebody, why he could tell where the Blue Robin was."

"Can't they find the first somebody?" asked Portulacca.

"I guess he died before people were born," said Poppy. Then he went on and told Petunia and

Portulacca how there was a wonderful blue stone in the King's crown, which was unlike all other precious stones, and said to be the Blue Robin's egg; and how there was a little Blue Book in the King's library which had a strange verse in it about the Blue Robin.

Then Poppy repeated the verse. He had learned it at school. It ran in this way:

"He who loveth me alone,
  Can tell me not from stick or stone;
  He who loveth more than me,
  Shall me in fullest glory see."

"What does that mean?" asked Petunia and Portulacca.

"I don't know," replied Poppy. Then he mended faster than ever. Many children ran past the window, hunting the Blue Robin, but he did not complain, even to himself.

That night his father did not come home, and Pink and Phlox cried as usual, and he had to rock them, and trot them. About midnight, however, they both fell asleep in their cradles, and Poppy began to think he might get a little rest himself. He could scarcely keep his eyes open. Petunia and Portulacca had been sound asleep in their cribs ever since seven o'clock.

Everything was very still, and he was just dozing, when he heard a sound which made him start up wide awake at once, although the children never stirred. He heard a single sweet bird-pipe, sweeter than anything he had ever heard in his life, and it seemed to be right in the room at his elbow. When the babies fell asleep Poppy had blown out the candle, the hearth-fire had gone out, and the room had been very dark, but now something was shining on the table like a lamp, which gave out a wonderful blue light. The sweet pipe came again. Poppy stared at the blue light on the table, which grew brighter and brighter, until he saw what it was. The Blue Robin shone on his table like a living sapphire, its blue wings seeming to fan the blue light into flames, its blue breast brighter than anything he had ever seen.

While all the world was out searching for the Blue Robin, it had come of its own accord to the poor little faithful boy in his poor little home.

The children all slept soundly, and did not stir. Poppy stood up trembling, and went over to the table, and immediately the Blue Robin flew to his hand, and clung there.

Then Poppy went out of the house, and down the road to the King's palace with the Blue Robin on his hand. Although it was so late, scarcely

227

anybody had gone to bed. They were all out with lanterns, hunting for the Blue Robin.

When Poppy with the Blue Robin on his hand came in sight, all the lanterns went out.

"What is that?" the people cried, "what is that wonderful blue light?"

They crowded around Poppy.

Then all of a sudden they shouted, "Poppy has found the Blue Robin! Poppy has found the Blue Robin!" and followed him to the King's Palace.

The shouts were heard in the newspaper office where Poppy's father was hard at work, and he ran to the window. When he saw his son with the Blue Robin, he was overwhelmed with joy. He stuck his pen behind his ear and came down on the fire-escape, and also went to the palace. The King had not gone to bed, though it was so late, neither had the Queen. They were talking about the Blue Robin and the perilous state of the country with the Prime Minister, on the front door-step.

When they saw Poppy and the blue Robin, and all the people, and heard the shouts of joy, the King tossed his crown in the air, the Prime Minister swung his hat, and the Queen ran in and wrapped up the Princess Honey in a little yellow silk gown, and brought her to see the wonderful sight.

It was wonderful—the Blue Robin on Poppy's hand seemed to light the whole city. Poppy, by the King's order, stood on the top door-step, and everybody could see the bird on his hand. Then the Blue Robin began to sing, and sang an hour without ceasing, so loud that everybody could hear.

When the bird stopped singing, the King advanced. "You shall now receive your reward," he said to Poppy, "and I will take the Blue Robin, and put him in a golden cage, and have him guarded by a regiment of picked soldiers."

The King extended his hand and Poppy his, but just as the King touched the Blue Robin, he disappeared. There came a faint song from far above the city roofs, and people tipped back their heads, and strained their eyes, but they could not see the Blue Robin; they never saw him again, as long as they lived.

However, he had been seen by many witnesses, and the object of the search was attained. There were no longer two parties in parliament, and the country was in a state of perfect peace. Indeed, parliament only met afterward to agree, and eat cake and ice cream, and shake hands.

Poppy had his reward at once—that is, everything but the hand of the Princess Honey—and he and his father and his little brothers and sisters, were very rich and happy, until he grew to be a man. Then the Princess Honey had grown to be a beautiful maiden, and he married her with great pomp, and the King gave them the Blue Robin's egg for a wedding-present.

MARY WILKINS FREEMAN.

By the Courtesy of the Author.

SOME PERFECT FAIRY STORIES

CHAPTER XII

MAKING OVER STORIES

THE average story must be cut and fitted to meet the needs of the story teller who wants to make a direct and vivid appeal to her children. Writing a story for the printed page and preparing a story for children's ears are two very different matters. In the former case, there is no time limit set upon the story; the reader may lay his story book down at will when he tires of the printed words, ready to take it up again when he has the inclination. In the latter case, we have to meet the mental and emotional needs of a group of children whose attention must be held by the compelling power of an orally delivered story. To meet these story needs as applied to oral delivery, a story has, ordinarily, to be made over before it is told. It must be made into a perfectly fitting garment for wrapping the child about with a clinging cloak of imagination, full of colorful words and truth. The story teller must do this story adapting herself. How can she bring it about in the quickest, most effectual way?

A large percentage of the stories printed for children are *too long*. The story that is too short and needs to be "padded" for telling is very rarely to be found. In the case of the Fables of Æsop and Bidpai the skeleton only of each story is given and here the problem of adapting for the story teller is to find a way of filling in each picture in order to make the story of the desired length.

But how shall we shorten the too-long story that we want children to hear because of its compelling theme and *motif,* but which is, very likely, two thousand or twenty-five hundred words long? This is the average difficulty that the story teller meets in connection with the average story. There is also the *time* problem to be taken into consideration, as well. While the story teller wants to spend as much time as necessary in the preparation of a story, this time ought to be reduced to a minimum. Is there a short cut to story adaptation and how may the story teller find it?

One may almost reduce a recipe for making over stories. It is possible to outline a pattern by means of which a printed story may be cut to fit the needs of a group of eager, restless, wriggling children. Having this recipe, this pattern, thoroughly in mind, a little practice in applying it to particular stories that need adapting will give the story teller power to apply it, quickly and effectually to any story with little loss of time. Its use will give the story teller an added power in her work. Knowing how to put stories in shape for telling will help her to hold the attention of any group of children.

The first step in our rule for adapting a story that is too long is to carefully *read the story*.

This seems too obvious a suggestion, almost, to put upon a printed page, but reading a story having in mind making it over means reading it to find out *what happens* in the story, *what is its important action, who are its necessary*

233

characters, and *what is the climax.* This first reading of a story for adaptation means an analysis of the story plot. This kind of story reading may be developed so as to become the story teller's habit in reading any story, but it is the necessary, preliminary step in all story adapting.

Our next step is to *find the pictures in the story.*

Suppose you were a stage manager with the problem of dramatizing this special story to meet the interests of an audience, how would you develop the different scenes in the story so as to make it into a play that holds interest? Suppose you are a film maker. What are the moving pictures in the story to be presented in their order of interest through the medium of your film? We have much to learn from the stage manager and the moving picture man. Their problems are identical with those of the story teller in that they must strip a story plot bare of details, unnecessary description and the opinions of the author. They must give an audience the *naked story.* This is all the audience wants. So it is with children. They demand story *scenes,* story *pictures* and nothing else.

The third and last step in story adaptation, is to *prepare our story pictures for presentation to the children.*

This step depends a good deal upon the children for whom you are preparing the story. If the children are foreign-born, you will need to put each story picture into a frame of very simple language. If yours are country children, you will need to put country images into the picture canvas. If they are city children, the canvas may need a few fire engines, parks and policemen to catch the children's attention. These will be, of course, quite subsidiary to the real story interest which must be preserved at all events.

It depends, also, upon the person who wrote the story. If we are adapting Hans Christian Andersen, Charles Dickens, Eugene Field or any other master story teller for the special needs of our story group, we must use the utmost care in keeping the *form* of the author and preserving his marvellous English. Too often the story teller ruins a story in attempting to "tell it down" to children. It is possible to shorten a good story and still keep it the author's own. It depends, most of all, upon determining the elements of *action, dialogue* and *description* necessary to make the story picture a fixture in the child's mind. Children want to know "what happens" in each scene of the story. This constitutes all their interest.

These, to sum up, are our steps in story adaptation:

Read the story, analytically.

Select its necessary scenes.

Reduce these scenes to elements of action.

We shall find it helpful to apply these separate steps to some one special story which we wish to present to children and which is too long for our use.

There is no more beautiful story in all literature than Hans Christian Andersen's "The Girl Who Trod on the Loaf." It is full of the sensory appeal, the colorful word picturing, the imagery, the ethics which we look for in a perfect story, but as it stands in the best translation, it is almost three thousand words long and so hedged about with Andersen's beautiful, but adult philosophy that it is quite beyond the comprehension of children. As a result, it is seldom told to children and is one of the least well-known of the author's fairy tales. Let us see if we can put it in shape for telling without, in the slightest degree, hurting Andersen's style.

We read the story analytically and find that it divides itself into four scenes, all of which are necessary to preserve the story interest. These are:

1. Inge's sinning.

2. Inge's descent to the abode of the Moor Woman.

3. Inge's repentance and transformation into the bird.

4. The bird's Christmas work and journey.

This analysis strips the story bare of detail. Each of these scenes, in the original story, is elaborated, split up into minor scenes, and they cover a very long period of time, which makes the story difficult for a child to understand. But if we keep carefully in mind these four separate pictures into which the story resolves itself and fill each picture with as little description as possible and only the essential action for carrying children by the quickest possible route to the climax, we find ourselves equipped with a new, shorter story, told in Andersen's words and ready for retelling to our children.

It will be well to compare this adapted version of the story as it appears here with the original story to be found in any translation of Hans Christian Andersen's stories to determine the omitted description, action and detail. The method of adapting this story is a model for other story adapting.

The Girl Who Trod on the Loaf

The girl's name was Inge; she was a poor child, but proud and presumptuous.

With years she grew worse rather than better.

She was sent into the country, in service, in the house of a rich people who kept her as their own child, and dressed her in corresponding style. She looked well, and her presumption increased.

When she had been there about a year, her mistress said to her, "You ought once to visit your parents, Inge.

"I'll make you a present of a great wheaten loaf that you may give to them; they will certainly be glad to see you again."

And Inge put on her best clothes, and her new shoes, and drew her skirts around her, and set out, stepping very carefully that she might be clean and neat about the feet; and there was no harm in that. But when she came to the place where the footway led across the moor, and where there were mud and puddles, she threw the loaf into the mud, and trod upon it to pass over without wetting her feet.

But as she stood there with one foot upon the loaf and the other uplifted to step farther, the loaf sank with her, deeper and deeper, till she disappeared altogether, and only a great puddle, from which the bubbles rose, remained where she had been.

Whither did Inge go? She sank into the moor ground, and went down to the Moor Woman, who is always brewing there. The Moor Woman is cousin to the Elf Maidens, who are well enough known, of whom songs are sung, and whose pictures are painted; but concerning the Moor Woman it is only known that when the meadows steam in summer-time, it is because she is brewing.

Into the Moor Woman's place did Inge sink down; and no one can endure that place long. A box of mud is a palace compared with the Moor Woman's brewery. Every barrel there has an odor that almost takes away one's senses; and the barrels stand close to each other; and wherever there is a little opening among them, through which one might push one's way, the passage becomes impracticable from the number of damp toads and fat snakes who sit out their time there. Among this company did Inge fall! and she shuddered and became stark and stiff.

She continued fastened to the loaf and the loaf drew her down as an amber button draws a fragment of straw.

That was a never ending antechamber where Inge found herself. There was a whole crowd of sinful people there, too. Great, fat, waddling spiders spun webs of a thousand years over the people's feet, webs that cut like wire and bound them like bronze fetters. Inge felt a terrible pain while she had to stand there as a statue, for she was tied fast to the loaf. Her clothes had been soiled with mud in coming down to the Moor Woman's place; a snake was fastened in her hair and out of each fold in her muddy frock a great toad looked forth, croaking.

The worst of all was the terrible hunger that tormented her. But could she not stoop and break off a piece of the loaf on which she stood? No, her back was too stiff, her hands and arms were benumbed, and her whole body was like a pillar of stone; only she was able to turn her eyes in her head, to turn them quite round, so that she could see backwards.

"If this lasts much longer," she said, "I shall not be able to bear it."

But she had to bear it, and it lasted on and on.

Her mother and all on earth knew of the sin she had committed; knew that she had trodden upon the loaf, and had sunk and disappeared; for the cowherd had seen it from the hill beside the moor.

And then she heard how her story was told to the little children, and the little ones said that she was so naughty and ugly that she must be well punished.

But one day when Inge was very hungry, she heard her name mentioned and her story was told to an innocent child. The little girl burst into tears at the tale of the haughty, vain Inge.

"But will Inge never come up here again?" asked the little girl.

And the reply was, "She will never come up again."

"But if she were to say she was sorry, and to beg pardon, and say she would never do so again?"

"Yes, then she might come," was the reply, and the words penetrated to Inge's heart and did her good, and a tear of penitence dropped down on the loaf.

Again time went on—a long, bitter time, but at last Inge heard some one call her name and she saw two bright stars that seemed gleaming above her. The little girl who had been sorry for Inge was now an old woman and had gone to Heaven. She was calling to Inge. She was still sorry for her.

And a wonderful thing happened. A beam of light shot radiantly down into the depths of the Moor Woman's place with all the force of the sunbeam which melts the snow man the boys have built. More quickly than the snowflake turns to water, the stony form of Inge was changed to mist, and a little bird soared with the speed of lightning upward into the world of men. But the bird was timid and shy towards all things around; he was ashamed of himself, ashamed to encounter any living thing, and hurriedly sought to conceal himself in a dark hole in an old crumbling wall; there he sat cowering, trembling through his whole frame.

Then, presently, it was the blessed Christmas time.   The peasant who dwelt near set up a pole by the old wall with some ears of corn bound to the top, that the birds of heaven might have a good meal, and rejoice in the happy, blessed time.

And on Christmas morning the sun arose and shone upon the ears of corn, which were surrounded by a number of twittering birds.   Then out of the hole in the wall streamed forth the voice of another bird, and the bird soared forth from his hiding-place; and in heaven it was well known what bird this was.

It was a hard winter.   The ponds were covered with ice, and the beasts of the field and the birds of the air were stinted for food.   Our little bird soared away over the high road, and in the ruts of the sledges he found here and there a grain of corn, and at the halting-places some crumbs.   Of these he ate only a few, but he called all the other hungry sparrows around him, that they, too, might have some food.   He flew into the towns, and looked round about; and wherever a kind hand had strewn bread on the window-sill for the birds, he only ate a single crumb himself, and gave all the rest to the other birds.

In the course of the winter, the bird had collected so many bread-crumbs, and given them to the other birds, that they equalled the weight of the loaf on which Inge had trod to keep her shoes clean; and when the last bread-crumb had been found and given, the gray wings of the bird became white, and spread far out.

"Yonder is a sea-swallow, flying away across the water," said the children, when they saw the white bird. Now it dived into the sea, and now it rose again into the clear sunlight. It gleamed white; but no one could tell whither it went, though some asserted that it flew straight into the sun.

Adapted from Hans Christian Andersen.

CHAPTER XIII

PLANNING STORY GROUPS

THE children who hear one story well told eagerly demand,

"Tell us another!"

It is the natural, to-be-desired longing of the child mind to be satiated with good stories. We endeavor to meet the children's wish for a number of stories in each story hour but we often hurt the mental and moral effect of one story by telling in close connection another story that has no interest connection with the last one told. We lead the child from one story interest to another with slight attention to the influence which the *story group* will have upon the minds of the children. We tell, perhaps, a home story, then a nature story, and last of all a holiday story in one story hour, and in doing this we so quickly transfer the child's attention from one theme to a distinctly different one that there is no cohesion in our story building. We break down instead of building up the powers of concentration of our children.

Planning a group of stories for one story hour is quite as much a matter to be studied as is the selection of each individual story in the group and preparing this story for telling. The story combination selected by the story teller must have the qualities of cohesion, unity of theme, and related interests .to make the story hour valuable in the child's life. On the other hand, the unity of theme in the separate stories chosen must be emphasized by contrasting story treatment of this central theme. A group of stories in which each story is just like its predecessor and similar to the story that follows will tire the child listeners. We must bring about cohesion in the story hour by means of contrast in the treatment of each story.

Our first thought in planning story groups will be:

Select the story theme for the story hour.

This story theme will be some idea which we want to bring forcefully to the minds of our children. The story hour *motif* may be: animals, the home, trades, birds, flowers, heroes, a holiday or some ethical theme as: honesty, truth or charity, but each of the stories selected for the story group will have an animal, home, trade, bird, flower, hero, holiday, honesty, truth or charity theme.

Our second thought in planning story groups will be:

Select stories which present the selected theme in contrasting treatment.

Three stories form an excellent number for one story hour. Each of these stories will illustrate one central idea that a *continuing thread of interest* may be carried through the story group and knotted at the end of the story hour. But each story will make a *different mental appeal in presenting the theme* that the children may have the benefit of *contrast* in helping them to concentrate upon listening to all the stories that make up the group.

The first of these three stories should be selected having in mind the securing of the *involuntary attention* of the children. It should be an *apperceptive* story that finds quick interpretation in the minds of the children because its ideas are *their* ideas, its scenes are familiar to theirs and its characters are people like the people whom they meet and know in their everyday environment. Having caught the children's attention involuntarily by a story that finds a place by its familiarity of treatment in their own lives, the second story in the group may make a different mental appeal. It may make the children *reason;* it may take them far afield in their thinking, it may be the longest story in the group and so call for greater concentration on the part of the story teller.

The last story in the story group will be selected for *mental relaxation* after the tense attention demanded for the second story. It may be a humorous story, a very short story, or one so contrasted in treatment to the other stories in the group that it gives rest because of its difference.

To illustrate with one typical story group will be helpful.

We wish to make the thought of *industry* the central thought for a story hour. The first story in the story group might be "The Sailor Man" by Laura E. Richards. This story catches and holds the children's attention at once because its characters are familiar to them; its setting is one that they can quickly see in their imagination. They have much in common with the two children who go to visit the sailor man; they know sailors; they have been to the seashore; they have enjoyed boat rides. And the climax of the story is a lesson in industry. The child who most industriously ties knots in the sailor's fish nets wins the reward.

The second story in the group, "The Stone in the Road," makes the children think more forcefully than did the first one. It takes them farther afield and makes them see in imagination, wealth, a castle, gold, poverty. They are obliged to reason in interpreting the rich man's motive in hiding his gold. The story makes the children use their dawning power of judging.

The last story selected for this special story group is, "Drakesbill," a humorous folk tale. The hero, an industrious duck who has worked hard all his life to accumulate a competence upon which he may live in his old age, loans a large sum of money to the king. The king being slow in paying back the money, Drakes-bill goes to the palace to collect his debt. His adventures on the way and the successful end of his journey form the interest of the story. This story makes a fine climax to the story group. While it still emphasizes the central thought of the story program, industry, it treats it in a different way from that in which the previous stories illuminate the theme. Its fantasy, its humor make it a relaxation for the children.

If story groups are arranged having in mind these two considerations: *a central theme* and *contrast in the treatment of this theme* the story hour will be a vital force for good in the development of the children's mental and moral life.

For the benefit of the story teller who has slight time for the consulting of many books of stories which such a planning of story groups entails, some illustrative story pro-grams follow, each of which has been arranged with reference to one child-interest theme carried through three different types of stories.

STORY PROGRAMS SELECTED BECAUSE OF THE PSYCHOLOGICAL APPEAL OF EACH GROUP

HOME PROGRAMS

The Home:
HOW THE HOME WAS BUILT
Maud Lindsay, in Mother Stories
THE LITTLE GRAY GRANDMOTHER
Elizabeth Harrison, in For the Children's Hour
THE SHEEP AND THE PIG   *Scandinavian Folk Tale*
The Kitchen:
THE LITTLE RED HEN   *Folk Tale*
THE TWO LITTLE COOKS
Laura E. Richards, in Five Minute Stories
THE WONDERFUL TEA KETTLE   *In Tales of Laughter*
Toys:
THE CHINA RABBIT FAMILY   *In In the Child's World*
THE TOP AND THE BALL   *Hans Christian Andersen*
THE DOLL IN THE GRASS   *In The Fairy Ring*
Being Neat:
THE CHILD WHO FORGOT TO WASH HIS FACE
Carolyn Sherwin Bailey, in Story Telling Time
DUST UNDER THE RUG   *Maud Lindsay, in Mother Stories*
THE PIG BROTHER
Laura E. Richards, in The Golden Windows
Cake:
THE CHRISTMAS CAKE
Maud Lindsay, in More Mother Stories

252

A Dog of Flanders   *Ouida*
The Dog in the Manger   *In Æsop's Fables*

The Horse:

The Little Gray Pony   *Maud Lindsay, in Mother Stories*
The Horse That Believed He'd Get There
                Annie Trumbull Slosson, in Story Tell Lib
A Wise Old Horse   *In In the Child's World*

The Cow:

The Friendly Cow
    Robert Louis Stevenson, in A Child's Garden of Verse
Irmgard's Cow   *Maud Lindsay, in More Mother Stories*
The Story the Milk Told Me
          Gertrude H. Noyes, in In the Child's World

The Rabbit:

Raggylug
    *Ernest Thompson Seton, adapted by Sara Cone Bryant,
      in Best Stories to Tell to Children*
Peter Rabbit   *Beatrix Potter*
Bre'r Rabbit and the Little Tar Baby
    Joel Chandler Harris, in Nights With Uncle Remus

The Squirrel:

The Thrifty Squirrels
           Mary Dendy, in In the Child's World
Squirrel Nutkin   *Beatrix Potter*
Bobby Squirrel's Busy Day
        Carolyn Sherwin Bailey, in Story Telling Time

Sheep:

Grandfather's Little Lamb
             In Stories and Rhymes for a Child
The Good Shepherd   *The Bible*
The Shepherd Boy and the Wolf   *In Æsop's Fables*

The Pig:

The Story of the Three Little Pigs
              In For the Children's Hour
The Little Pig   *Maud Lindsay, in More Mother Stories*

FOR THE STORY TELLER

THE STARS   *Laura E. Richards, in The Golden Windows*

HOW THE SUN, THE MOON, AND THE WIND WENT OUT TO
     DINNER   *In Tales of Laughter*

Apples:

THE SLEEPING APPLE   *In In the Child's World*

THE BIG RED APPLE
     Kate Whiting Patch, in For the Children's Hour

APPLE SEED JOHN   *In Saint Nicholas Files*

The Barnyard:

THE GOOSE THAT LAID GOLDEN EGGS   *Old Folk Tale*

THE UGLY DUCKLING   *Hans Christian Andersen*

A BARNYARD TALK
     Emilie Poulsson, in In the Child's World

Light:

THE OLD STREET LAMP   *Hans Christian Andersen*

THE GOLDEN WINDOWS
     Laura E. Richards, in The Golden Windows

THE MOON CAKE   *In Tales of Laughter*

Snow:

THE SNOW MAN   *Hans Christian Andersen*

GRANDFATHER'S PENNY   *In For the Children's Hour*

HOW PETER RABBIT GOT HIS WHITE PATCH
     Thornton Burgess, in Mother West Wind's Children

Water:

THE LITTLE HERO OF HARLEM
     *Adapted by Sara Cone Bryant, in Best Stories to Tell
     to Children*

TOM, THE WATER BABY
     Charles Kingsley, adapted in For the Children's Hour

WHY THE SEA IS SALT   *In Tales of Laughter*

Leaves:

THE ANXIOUS LEAF
     Henry Ward Beecher, in For the Children's Hour

THE MAPLE LEAF AND THE VIOLET
     Eugene Field, in A Little Book of Profitable Tales

THE SNOWFLAKE AND THE LEAF
     Helen Preble, in For the Children's Hour

FOR THE STORY TELLER

The Bee:

    LITTLE BEE TRUNKHOSIE   *In Firelight Stories*

    THE BEE MAN OF ORNE

                Frank R. Stockton, in Fanciful Tales

    BATTLE OF THE MONKEY AND THE CRAB

             Japanese Fairy Tale, in Tales of Laughter

Trees:

    THE LITTLE PINE TREE THAT WISHED FOR NEW LEAVES

                In For the Children's Hour

    OLD PIPES AND THE DRYAD

                Frank R. Stockton, in Fanciful Tales

    THE THREE LITTLE CHRISTMAS TREES THAT GREW ON THE

    HILL   *Mary McDowell, in The Story Teller's Book*

TRADE PROGRAMS

The Farmer:

    THE LARKS IN THE CORN FIELD   *In Æsop's Fables*

    DO WHAT YOU CAN   *In For the Children's Hour*

    THE FARMER AND THE TROLL   *In Tales of Laughter*

The Baker:

    NERO AT THE BAKERY

             Emilie Poulsson, in In the Child's World

    THE QUEER LITTLE BAKER MAN

        Phila Butler Bowman, in Mother's Magazine, November, 1912

    THE OLD WOMAN WHO LOST HER DUMPLINGS

                In Tales of Laughter

The Shoemaker:

    GOODY TWO SHOES

              Emilie Poulsson, see page 16

    THE ELVES AND THE SHOEMAKER   *Grimm*

    THE HOP-ABOUT MAN   *In The Story Teller's Book*

The Blacksmith:

    THE LITTLE GRAY PONY

            Maud Lindsay, in Mother Stories

    VULCAN   *In In the Child's World*

    THE VILLAGE BLACKSMITH   *Longfellow*

PLANNING STORY GROUPS

HOLIDAY PROGRAMS

Thanksgiving:
HOW PATTY GAVE THANKS   *In In the Child's World*
THE STORY OF THE FIRST THANKSGIVING
      Nora Archibald Smith, in The Story Hour
THE PUMPKIN GLORY
      William Dean Howells, in Christmas Every Day

Christmas:
THE NIGHT BEFORE CHRISTMAS   *Clement Moore*
THE LEGEND OF CLAUS
      Eugene Field, in A Little Book of Profitable Tales
THE GOLDEN COBWEBS   *In Best Stories to Tell to Children*

Easter:
AN EASTER SURPRISE.
      Louise M. Oglevee, in Story Telling Time
A LESSON IN FAITH
      Margaret Gatty, in In the Child's World
HERR OSTER HAASE   *In For the Children's Hour*

Stories of Patriotism:
HOW CEDRIC BECAME A KNIGHT
      Elizabeth Harrison, in For the Children's Hour
LITTLE GEORGE WASHINGTON
      Nora Archibald Smith, in The Story Hour
THE LAST LESSON
      Adapted by Sara Cone Bryant, in How to Tell Stories
      to Children.

For a Birthday:
THE BIRTHDAY PRESENT
      Maud Lindsay, in More Mother Stories
DICKY SMILEY'S BIRTHDAY
      Nora Archibald Smith, in The Story Hour
THE BIRTHDAY PARTY
      Gertrude Smith, in The Story Teller's Book

FOR THE STORY TELLER

ETHICAL PROGRAMS

Being Brave:
THE EYES OF THE KING
          Carolyn Sherwin Bailey, in Story Telling Time
THE LITTLE HERO OF HARLEM
          Sara Cone Bryant, in Best Stories to Tell to Children
THE BRAVE TIN SOLDIER   *Hans Christian Andersen*

Being Industrious:
THE SAILOR MAN
          Laura Richards, in The Golden Windows
THE STONE IN THE ROAD   *In For the Children's Hour*
DRAKESBILL   *In The Story Teller's Book*

Being Kind:
THE LITTLE BROWN LADY
          Phila Butler Bowman, in Story Telling Time
THE WHEAT FIELD
          Laura E. Richards, in The Golden Windows
LITTLE HALF CHICK   *In For the Children's Hour*

Being Generous:
THE LITTLE BOY WHO HAD A PICNIC
          Carolyn Sherwin Bailey, in Stories and Rhymes for a Child.
THE HAPPY PRINCE   *Oscar Wilde*
THE LITTLE OLD MAN AND HIS GOLD
          Phila Butler Bowman, in Story Telling Time

Being Hospitable:
THE SELFISH GIANT
          Oscar Wilde, in The Happy Prince and Other Fairy Tales.
BAUCIS AND PHILEMON
          Adapted in For the Children's Hour
THE WOODPECKER WHO WAS SELFISH, *see page 181*

Being Honest:
THE LITTLE COWHERD BROTHER
          In Story Telling in School and Home

PLANNING STORY GROUPS

The Honest Woodman   *In In the Child's World*
The Street Musicians   *In The Story Teller's Book*

MISCELLANEOUS PROGRAMS

Good Little Folk:
The Adventures of a Brownie *(to be adapted)*
                                   Miss Mulock
The One-Footed Fairy   *Alice Brown*
The Gradual Fairy
               Alice Brown, in The One-Footed Fairy

Funny Stories:
The Story of Lambikin   *In Firelight Stories*
The Happy Family   *Hans Christian Andersen*
The Story of Little Black Mingo
               Helen Bannerman, in Tales of Laughter

Myths:
The Paradise of Children
               In Myths Every Child Should Know
The Story of Persephone   *In For the Children's Hour*
The Golden Touch
          Adapted, in Myths Every Child Should Know

Fairy Animals:
The Winding Up Place *(to be adapted)*
                              In Mopsa The Fairy
The Chimæra *(to be adapted)*
               In Myths Every Child Should Know
The Little Jackal and the Alligator
               In Best Stories to Tell to Children

Princesses:
The Crown
          Carolyn Sherwin Bailey, in Story Telling Time
The Princess and the Pea   *Hans Christian Andersen*
The Princess Whom Nobody Could Silence
                              In Tales of Laughter

259

VALUABLE REFERENCE BOOKS FOR THE STORY TELLER

How to Tell Stories to Children	*Sara Cone Bryant*
Stories to Tell to Children	*Sara Cone Bryant*
The Children's Reading	*Frances Jenkins Olcott*
Story Telling: What to Tell and How to Tell It	
	Edna Lyman

A LIST OF GOOD STORIES TO TELL TO CHILDREN UNDER TWELVE YEARS OF AGE

Index to Short Stories	*Salisbury and Beckwith*
The Story in Early Education	*Sara Wiltse*
Story Telling in School and Home	*Partridge*
The Story Teller's Book	*Alice O'Grady and Frances Throop*
Story Telling Time	*Frances Weld Danielson*
In the Child's World	*Emilie Poulsson*
For the Children's Hour	*Bailey and Lewis*
Mother Stories	*Maud Lindsay*
More Mother Stories	*Maud Lindsay*
Tales of Laughter	
	Kate Douglas Wiggin and Nora Archibald Smith
The Talking Beasts	
	Kate Douglas Wiggin and Nora Archibald Smith
Story-Tell Lib	*Annie Trumbull Slosson*
The Golden Windows	*Laura E. Richards*
The Story Hour	
	Kate Douglas Wiggin and Nora Archibald Smith
Stories and Rhymes for a Child	*Carolyn Sherwin Bailey*
Firelight Stories	*Carolyn Sherwin Bailey*
The Wonder Book	*Nathaniel Hawthorne*
Tanglewood Tales	*Nathaniel Hawthorne*
Fairy Tales	*The Brothers Grimm*
" "	*Hans Christian Andersen*
" "	*Joseph Jacobs*

PLANNING STORY GROUPS

THE ONE-FOOTED FAIRY	*Alice Brown*
THE BOSTON COLLECTION OF KINDERGARTEN STORIES	
THE CHILDREN'S HOUR	*Eva March Tappan*
THE JUNGLE BOOKS	*Rudyard Kipling*
THE JUST SO STORIES	*Rudyard Kipling*
NATURE MYTHS	*Florence Holbrook*
THE HAPPY PRINCE AND OTHER FAIRY TALES	*Oscar Wilde*
WHY THE CHIMES RANG	*R. M. Alden*
NIGHTS WITH UNCLE REMUS	*Joel Chandler Harris*
JOHNNY CROW'S GARDEN	*Leslie Brooke*
GRANNY'S WONDERFUL CHAIR	*Francis Browne*
PARABLES FROM NATURE	*Margaret Gatty*
FORGOTTEN TALES OF LONG AGO	*E. V. Lucas*
THE BOOK OF CHRISTMAS	*Hamilton W. Mabie*
MYTHS EVERY CHILD SHOULD KNOW	*Hamilton W. Mabie*
HEROES EVERY CHILD SHOULD KNOW	*Hamilton W. Mabie*
MOPSA THE FAIRY	*Jean Ingelow*
THE DOG OF FLANDERS AND OTHER STORIES	*Ouida (Ramée)*
THE CHILDREN'S BOOK	*Horace E. Scudder*
THE BEE-MAN OF ORNE	*Frank R. Stockton*
HALF A HUNDRED HERO TALES	*Francis Storr*
STORIES AND POEMS FOR CHILDREN	*Celia Thaxter*